SINKIN SPELLS, HOT FLASHES, FITS AND CRAVINS

*"You got the good ingredient,
You got the good thing."*

— Aunt Emma

SINKIN SPELLS, HOT FLASHES, FITS AND CRAVINS

Ernest Matthew Mickler

With Color Photographs by the Author

 Ten Speed Press

Design by Jonathan Greene (*Gnomon Press, Frankfort, Kentucky*)
Setting by Graphic Composition, Inc. (*Athens, Georgia*)

Cover art by the author, cover design by Brent Beck

Collaboration with Gary Jolley

1☉
TEN SPEED PRESS
P O Box 7123
Berkeley, California 94707

I would like, again, to thank those who gave me their names as well as their recipes; and I would also like to thank those who gave me their recipes without their names. . . And a very special thank-you to Tom Meyer and Jonathan Williams, of the Jargon Society, Highlands, North Carolina, who tasted, sifted, shifted, and generally stirred the pot and brought it to a boil. I would also like to thank John Keasler from Ball Ground, Georgia and Cal Yeomans, Center, Florida.

E.M.M.

Library of Congress Cataloging-in-Publication Data

Mickler, Ernest Matthew

   1. Cookery, American—Southern style. I. Title.
II. Title: Sinkin Spells, Hot Flashes, Fits and Cravins.
TX715.M6334   1988   641.5975   88–24821
ISBN 0–89815–269–0 (cloth)
ISBN 0–89815–268–2 (spiral)

First Printing, 1988

Manufactured in the United States of America

1 2 3 4 5 6 — 93 92 91 90 89 88

*"It was the most magnannygoshus
day, ever. Edna Rae loved sayin that
when the weather was good. . . You
know as well as I do, if Edna Rae
hadn'ta been in that box, she'da been on
Saunders' Dock a-fishin."*

"I have never seen a sociological document of such beauty—the photographs alone are shattering. I shall treasure it always. . . Now that it's harder than ever to identify the genuine article on sight—with two generations of prosperity white trash looks like gentry—we've long needed something other than the ballot box to remind us of their presence: WHITE TRASH COOKING is a beautiful testament to a stubborn people of proud and poignant heritage."—Harper Lee (author of *To Kill a Mockingbird*)

". . . I read cookbooks like some people read music scores and I can hear the recipes sing! Most of them sound like pretty good eatin'. I *do* like the flavor of this book."—Vertamae Grosvenor ("All Things Considered," *NPR*)

"Perhaps the most intriguing book of the 1986 spring cookbook season is WHITE TRASH COOKING . . . this book is a delight to peruse. It is one of the few unvarnished regional cookbooks around."—Bryan Miller, *New York Times Book Review*

"You can't beat this book, not even with a Waring blender. It is a great missionary effort, introducing to the hordes of the well-washed such wonders as the Anti-Stick Peanut Butter Sandwich."—Richard Starr, *The Washington Times Magazine*

"WHITE TRASH COOKING is a marvelous and genuine book—not camp—because it sees clearly, without condescension. The food goes from awful with lots of 'oleo' to very good. The language sings throughout."—Barbara Kafka, *Vogue*

"How did you know that Trashin Cookin is my favorite of all cuisines? The French and Italians, aside from the peasants, can't begin to compete. I know I shall find many delights in this superb book."—J. William Fulbright, Former U.S. Senator from Arkansas

"That is the most delicious cookbook I have encountered—and it seems my diet in childhood was all White Trash! So many beloved old recipes have turned up. Bless you!"—Helen Hayes

CONTENTS

FAMILY REUNIONS, BARBEQUES, FISH FRYS, AND PICNICS   45

SEWIN, QUILTIN, TACKY
AND HOME DEMONSTRATION PARTIES   95

COVINA'S CLUTCH   97

SINKIN SPELLS, HOT
FLASHES, FITS AND CRAVINS   115

GREENS COVER A MULTITUDE OF SINS   117

EATIN ON THE GROUND   133

AUNT DOE RAE'S PACKAGED-UP WORLD   135

PREFACE

Is this just SON OF WHITE TRASH COOKING? Not really. Of course some people would like the sun to come up in the West and be bright green, just to make things 'different'.

This time Ernie Mickler, the nonpareil catbird of Moccasin Branch, Florida, makes us concentrate on all of the most sacred and secular ceremonies of the Very Deepest South. He first gives us eight stories (Roark Bradford and Joel Chandler Harris gave us black dialect like this a long time ago, but I can't think of anyone who has given us unvarnished white talk like this—perhaps ever). Gracie Dwiggers' account (over the phone) of Edna Rae's funeral and wake is a little Southern classic. . . And then we have more of his rococo-cocacola recipes (some are stunning, some are killing). . . And then we have a portfolio of 80 of Ernie's admirably simple and revealing snapshots. That's more than last time, because so many of his fans were so smitten by those natural images.

Whatever the policies and sleazy confusions of the 1980s in America, there is a national groundswell that insists that we pay attention to our marvelous diversity. Whether it is the plain, tasty cooking of the Geechee islands; or the paintings of the late Sam Doyle, of Frogmore, SC; or Shaker chairs and lemon pie in Kentucky, we are getting to like ourselves just a bit more. "We Ain't Nuthin But A Hound Dog!"—why should we be anything but? It's been a stray-dog country ever since the Garden of Eden got chewed up and spit out.

For those of you who just paid $129.50 (plus tip) for three in a silly, pink, revolting, state-of-the-fart, yupped-up, urbane restrunt, may we offer you a walk on the rustic road to the Palace of Wisdom? Bring your Gaviscon, your Metamucil—and your spirits, way up high! SINKIN SPELLS, HOT FLASHES, FITS AND CRAVINS is for those of us who are still US.

Jonathan Williams

FOOT WASHINS, PRAYER MEETINS, CREEK BAPTISMS, AND ALL DAY SINGS

CONNETTA'S DREAM

Lou May Witkins screeched to a halt right in front of Iris Maxine Dove's house. They were the best of friends and she couldn't wait to get inside and tell her the very latest. Lou May made a fast slide out of her car. She fixed herself up. Shifting here and there and a nonchalant pull at the back of her skirt to make sure the 'goat was not in the pasture'. Her friend was constantly reminding her of that. Iris had already parted the curtains and was watching.

But, by this time, Lou May had lost all her patience and started screaming Iris's name way back at the street. Iris met Lou May at the stoop and helped her get in quick, cause she could tell it was the 'low downest' piece she'd heard in a long time. Iris could always depend on Loumie (she called her that) to bring the very 'worst' right to her kitchen table. And Iris specially knew it was Thursdays, today, that Loumie had her regular weekly standing appointment at Oleen's Beauty Shop.

Loumie didn't even say hello, just rushed straight through to the kitchen and squirmed-down in a yellow-bottomed, pearlized dinette chair. Iris had already poured her a cup of strong coffee when Lou May said, "Iris, I've heard it all now. You cain jus go on an kill me and bury me cause I heard it all."

Iris, forgetting to compliment her on one of Oleen's finest hairdos and lavender-pearl rinse jobs, didn't play games or waste time. She asked her, straight out, which dryer she was under.

"I was under number three," Loumie said.

"That's the one which makes an awful racket. You cain't hear right, under that thing. Are you shore you heard it all, exactly?" Iris asked.

"Well, I finagled it until I got one of my ears free from it so as I didn't miss a word. But she HAD already started," Loumie said in a not-so-sure way.

"OH! Honey, your ear shows it too, it's red as fire," Iris came back.

"That ain't necessarily from the heat of the dryer, darlin, I want you to know that for shore," Loumie shot back just as quickly.

3

"Well I know who's there with you on Thursday, so it's got to be on Marrabelle Shuster." (Loumie's face didn't register.) "Or, Connetta Boyle." (Iris could tell that was the jackpot.)

"Iris you scare me. I think you got one of them see-all minds or something," Loumie said, kind of bewildered.

"An if it's about Connetta" Iris came right back, "it's got to be a good one. Cause you know what they say about anybody that gits her hair dyed that awful purple-red color, plus wearin them open-toed things on their feet. An what mother do you know, would let her young'uns go barefooted 'fore May 1st or 'fore the dew dries. She just beggin for ground-itch."

"Well, it's true and I know you're plenty right," Lou May said. "But I got to hand it to Oleen, she listened to the whole story and didn't flinch a hair. She even laughed a little. An I made positive that I kept my nose stuck in my National Enquirer. I helt it up so high there was noway they could see my free ear."

"Enough of the preliminaries, Loumie, now git own with it. You done flusstrated me," Iris piped.

"Just hold your taters, Iris," she said, and without further priming lit into the story:

"Well, it seems Connetta's been goin to that Holycostal Church over in Itta Bena, the one where they do everything from snake hanlin to speakin in farun tongues. And she told Oleen, right while she was dabbin at her roots, that this secret society had picked her to wash the preacher's feet right after the actin out of the Last Supper."

"Well . . . she does kinda look like that Mary Magdalene with all that hair an everything," Iris added. "But that secret society, I can tell you that was the preacher himself."

"Now, first of all, how do you know what Mary Magdalene looks like, and what makes you so shore the preacher's the picker all by hisself?" Lou May questioned.

"She's all over the Bible pitchers and she's in every play," Iris declared, "and they ain't many of 'em around that can turn down a chance like that. She's carryin a sign. . . . . them open-toed shoes. Plus that power them preachers has got over people, some just use it like the devil."

"I know you're right, but it just gripes me to think of it,"

Loumie squenched. "Enough of that. We'll do the judgin later on," she said, as she continued the story:

"About that time, Oleen chuckled when Connetta told her that the preacher suggested, since it was like a play, maybe they ought to have a little rehearsal on the side. I mean it was different from the rest of the thing, was her exact words she told Oleen. She said the preacher said she didn't need to bring a thing."

Iris broke in, "I bet he did. I wonder what he'd a done if she coulda left her you-know-what home. That woulda froze his monkey."

"Now be quiet, Iris, er you gone mess up the story," Loumie said before getting back to where she was:

"She told Oleen that she'd never been to a foot washin before and didn't know what on earth to expect. So she said she put a perfumed-up old washrag in a little baggie and stuck it down in her pocketbook just in case. An don't you dare say what you thinkin, Iris, the story's bad enough as is. She got to the church at the specified time, tried the door but it was locked. The preacher was right there though, so he let her in and relocked the door."

"I bet he did," Iris slipped in.

"Shut up Iris. Quit buttin in. I'm the one that overheard all this," Loumie said, kind of exasperated, but went on telling Iris, "It's a downright dirty dog rotten shame people's got to ack like that."

"Ack like what, darlin, you ain't told old Iris nothin yet?"

"Well, I hope to God I don't have to spell it out for you, cause I ain't usin the language Connetta used on poor Oleen," Loumie said.

"Poor Oleeeeeeen!!! Honey, she's heard everything they is to hear an then some, an take an turn that wrong-side-outereds an she's bared witness to that too," Iris ranted. "They hear it all from who's gotta itch where to who's a scratchin it —an with what!"

"Well, I've listened to it all now," Loumie continued:

"She told Oleen that it went fine and nothin much happened till they got right down to the ackshul washin of the preacher's feet. She said he had this big enamel basin filled up with water, sittin at the foot of a chair, square in the middle of the church platform. But he had his own washrag. So she didn't need to use hers. But when Connetta started washin at his feet, he beginned to laugh like a crazy man, an every time she felt of his feet he'd go goofy on er. It went on like that for a while and finally, she told Oleen, she just quit cause she couldn't hold on to his feet anyways. Then, he set off to outright beg her to tickle his feet some more. An she said he wasn't just askin, he was beeeeeeeggin, honey. At first, she said, she didn't. But he kept on pleadin at er till she couldn't stand it. So, she took that rag an worked . . . his . . . feet . . . over. She told Oleen she thought she'd have to get the okgegon tent to re-vive 'im."

Iris was squealing in her seat and Loumie knew she had her goin' so a little mischief at this point wouldn't hurt a thing:

"Right then, while she was wrenchin that mess outta her hair, Oleen asked er, at the real foot washin, not the rehearsal, what did them Itta Bena ladies bring to eat?" Loumie went on, taking the story to an abrupt turn.

Iris didn't stand still for it and said, as if she was going to choke Loumie, "You are pullin my leg! With Oleen's appetite for dirt, she'da never asked Connetta any such thing in the middle of that kinda story —or your hair ain't purple". . . . . "Oh God, I didn't mean that Loumie! I meant Connetta's hair. Yours is just a shade darker than it usually is."

But it didn't faze Loumie, because she had decided where she was going with the story, so she just went on with the list of dishes the ladies from the Itta Bena Holycostal Church had brought to the foot washin. "Connetta said they had greens and beans, corn breads and corn pones, dumplins, stews and casseroles. They had Spam, ham, an fried pork chops. Pies, cakes and a puddin or two."

"Okay, Loumie, we know what them ladies from Itta Bena eat, now git back to the story," Iris said hopefully.

Loumie, still with devilment, continued, "She told Oleen that about that time her and the preacher tumped over backwards and rolled and wiggled and squirmed all over that platform and, then, the preacher made his lunge. . . . ."

"Oh . . . my . . . god . . . Iris, is that clock right. I don't believe it. I got to git home and start my supper. I had no idea it was that late!" She grabbed her pocketbook and ran for the door.

Iris didn't move. But, she thought, if she could have gotten her hand on Lou May Witkins head, she'd have pulled all of her almost-purple hair out! But, instead, she'd have to call Oleen to get the rest of the story, even though they were still on the outs over another cross-wired story from under dryer number three.

AUNT SARAH'S STEPPED ON CORN BREAD

Alabama ground cornmeal
Enough hot water to make a mush
Plenty bacon drippings

Make pone. Bake 2 or 3 hours at 250 degrees.
Aunt Sarah said, "Careful you don't hurt your foot."

GAYNELL'S TATER TOES CASSEROLE

2 lbs ground beef
1 large onion, chopped
1 can Campbell's Cream
   of Mushroom Soup
1 can Campbell's Golden
   Mushroom Soup

1 soup can of water
1 2-lb package of Tater
   Tots or 2 1-lb
   packages

Fry down the beef and onion. Add the soup and water and mix thoroughly. Pour the Tater Tots over the top and cook at 475 degrees for 25 minutes.

Gaynell said, "This'll restore your energy after washin all them feet."

Serves 6.

AUNT JENNY'S COMPANY'S COMING CASSEROLE

1 lb ground beef
2 8-oz cans tomato sauce
½ lb cottage cheese
1 8-oz package of
　Philadelphia Cream
　Cheese, softened
¼ cup sour cream

⅓ cup green onions,
　chopped
2 or 3 Tbs chopped green
　pepper
2 Tbs melted butter
12 oz thick, flat noodles,
　cooked and drained

Cook the ground beef until browned. Stir in the tomato sauce. Combine cottage cheese, cream cheese, sour cream, green onions, green pepper. In a two-quart casserole spread half the noodles, cover with cheese mixture, then cover with the rest of the noodles. Pour on the melted butter, cover with the beef-tomato mixture and bake uncovered in a 375-degree oven for 30 minutes.

"Will serve as many as you can," she said.

FOOT POTATO SALAD

4 cups cooked potatoes,
　cut into chunks (if
　you lined 'em up it'd
　be about a foot of
　'em).
4 hard-boiled eggs,
　chopped
1½ cups sliced celery
¼ cup sliced radishes

½ cup sliced green
　onions, including
　green tops
1 cup mayonnaise, Kraft
1 Tbs apple cider vinegar
1½ tsp salt
2 tsp French's yellow
　mustard
½ tsp celery seed

Mix together the first five things. Thoroughly blend the mayonnaise, vinegar, mustard, celery seed, and salt. Pour over potatoes and mix with your hands. Chill and it carries good.

Serves 6.

TRUE GRITS CHILI

6 medium onions, chopped fine
6 medium green peppers, chopped fine
2 garlic cloves, minced
4 lbs ground beef
4 16-oz cans tomatoes with juice
5 16-oz cans kidney beans, drained
2 cups cooked grits
2 6-oz cans tomato paste
1 cup water
1 tsp apple cider vinegar
3 whole cloves
2 bay leaves
4 or 5 Tbs good chili powder (Maxene's, if you can get it)

In a skillet brown the onion, garlic, and peppers in oil until golden. In another skillet, brown the beef in batches. Drain off fat. Mix the beef and onion together in a large pot and add the tomatoes, beans, grits, tomato paste, water, salt, vinegar, cloves, chili powder, bay leaves, and black pepper, to taste. Cover and simmer one hour over low heat. Add a pinch of sugar. Simmer uncovered for another hour. Take out the bay leaves and cloves (hope you can find 'em all) before serving.

If it's right off the stove it'll say hot for an hour. Serves 20.

OLEEN'S STUFFED PEPPER SLIPPERS

8 green peppers
1 cup cooked rice
1 Tbs Crisco
1 lb ground beef
¼ cup chopped onion
¼ cup chopped green pepper
1½ tsp salt
½ tsp pepper

Cut tops off peppers and remove the pepper seeds. Put peppers into boiling water and cook 2 minutes—don't overcook. Drain. Melt Crisco in a skillet and add ground beef, onion, chopped pepper, salt and pepper. Brown and add rice and mix. Stuff peppers with mixture and place in baking dish and bake for 30 minutes in a 350-degree oven. Serves 8.

CONNETTA BOYLE'S COLE SLAW

1 head cabbage, shredded	½ cup bees' honey
1 onion, chopped	½ cup apple cider vinegar
1 green pepper, chopped	½ cup cooking oil
1 3-oz can pimientos	2 tsp sugar
	2 tsp salt

Mix together the cabbage, onion, pepper, and pimiento. Combine remaining ingredients in a pot and bring to a boil. Pour dressing over the cabbage mixture and mix well. Cover and refrigerate for 3 days.

Careful when you take the lid off, cause sometimes it'll smell like old feet.

Serves 10.

PRAYER MEETIN PUNCH

2 quarts of good sweetened tea	1 6-oz can frozen limeade
1 22-oz can canned orange juice	1 6-oz can frozen pink lemonade
1 6-oz can frozen pineapple juice	

To the tea, add the frozen juices and then stir in the orange juice. Chill and let sit till your throats are dry.

Serves 16.

PREACHER'S CHICKEN KETCHA-COLA

Fryer
Bottle of ketchup
Bottle of Coca-Cola

Cut up your chicken just like for frying and salt and pepper it a lot. Put all of it in a skillet at the same time. Cover it with a whole bottle of ketchup—the size hamburger stands have on the counters—then pour in a bottle of Coca-Cola (no substitutes, please) and cook it over medium heat till it's done. You can sorta flake meat off the bone with a fork when it's done and it looks like barbecue sauce. You can tell if it's not done by tasting it.

MOCCASIN BRANCH SKILLET CAKE

1½ cups flour
¾ cup Crisco oil
½ cup buttermilk
1 egg
2 tart cooking apples, peeled and sliced

2 tsp vanilla
1 cup pecans, chopped
1 cup sugar
1 tsp salt
1 tsp baking soda

Combine all the dry things in a big bowl. Add what's left and thoroughly mix. Grease up a cast iron skillet and pour in the batter. In a 350-degree oven cook for 40 to 50 minutes.

Tastes even better if you can dangle your feet in the branch while you're eatin it.

MARY MAGDALENE'S ARSH POTATER SALAD

1 lb cooked Arsh
   potaters, cubed
3 hard-boiled eggs,
   chopped
¼ cup ripe olives,
   chopped

3 Tbs green pepper,
   chopped
1 cup sliced celery
1 onion, diced
½ cup mayonnaise
2 Tbs French's mustard

Combine mayonnaise and mustard. Mix the other ingredients together and pour dressing over, mixing thoroughly. Season with salt and pepper to taste. Chill. Doubles and quadruples real good.
   Serves 4.

MARY LOU'S DEVILED-UP COLLARD GREEN SURPRISE

1 loaf corn pone or corn bread (a little smaller than a shoe box)
2 cups of leftover collards, including liquor and fatback
1 tsp yellow salad mustard

A. Scoop out center of corn pone. Reserve for corn bread and milk.

B. Dice fatback, if pieces are large and return to collards.

C. Mix collard greens, mustard and just enough of the pot liquor for a soggy but not soupy consistency.

D. Fill corn pone with the collard mixture. Let sit a few minutes, slice and serve.

POTTA COLLARDS

2 bunches of collards
Fatback or ham to season
Salt and pepper to taste

Pick out and strip the leaves from the tough stems. Wash 'em to death to get rid of the grit. Takes about 3 to 4 washings. Fry out the season meat till you get a little fat from it. Drop in the collards by the handful and cover. If pot is too small, fill it and let them wilt, then there's plenty of room for the rest. When all is wilted, add enough water to cover. If they a real strong greens and smell bitter pour off the first water and add more. That cuts down on the strong taste. Simmer till tender, add a pinch or two of sugar and cook ten more minutes.

HOT PEPPER CABBAGE

1 head cabbage
Season meat
3 hot peppers

Sear season meat and peppers in a dutch oven. Cut cabbage into quarters and add. Cover and cook till tender. 15 or 20 minutes. Add water if necessary.

OLEEN'S BEAUTY PARLOR POUND CAKE

1 cup Crisco
2½ cups plain flour, sifted
½ cup self-rising flour,
   sifted
2½ cups sugar
5 eggs
2 tsp vanilla
1 cup milk

Blend Crisco and sugar for 10 minutes. Add eggs one at a time. Beat each time for one minute. Add milk and vanilla and flour and blend well. Bake in tube pan for one hour at 325 degrees. If necessary, let cool.

MARY MAGDALENE'S NEVER FAIL POTATO ROLLS

1 pack yeast	2 eggs, beaten
1 cup milk, lukewarm	1 tsp salt
1½ lbs cooked potatoes	Flour
¼ cup shortening	2 tsp sugar

Dissolve yeast in lukewarm milk. Whip potatoes, add yeast, sugar, shortening, eggs and salt. Add enough flour to make a soft dough. Let rise till doubled in bulk. Roll out half inch thick and cut with biscuit cutter. Spread with butter and fold over. Let rise an hour and a half. Bake at 450 degrees for 10 to 12 minutes.

MT. NEBO MOCK LOBSTER SALAD

(No Seafood in Recipe)

¼ lb crackers	2 hard-boiled eggs, chopped
1 sweet green pepper, diced	2 cups tomato juice
1 cup celery, diced	1 cup mayonnaise

Crumble crackers, add remaining ingredients and mix. Tastes like lobster but there's none in it.

Crackers should be in rather large pieces.

SLUICEY-DAB IN A FOOT TUB

1 head lettuce, large	Salt and pepper
Duke's mayonnaise	1 large cucumber
Sour cream	1 large onion
Cider vinegar	1 good-sized tomato

Shred lettuce thinly. Thinly slice cucumber and onion. Chop up tomato coarsely. Throw together in a large bowl or foot tub. Add sour cream, mayonnaise and cider vinegar until the vegetables are covered probably about a quarter inch—the salad should be rather thin and "sluicey"—soupy. Amounts are probably about 2 pints mayonnaise to one half pint vinegar and one pint sour cream. (That's a guess.) Lots of salt and pepper to taste. You'll know when it's right. Runny, soupy, and wilted. It's better from the icebox. And even better left over on sandwiches.

STEAM FRIED CORN

Cut corn off cob. Brown bacon in cast iron skillet. Add corn and some water, at least 2 tablespoons, but no more than half a cup. Steam fry approximately 3 minutes on medium heat or until water is just about gone. Put a piece of tinfoil on it and in the cooter shell it goes.

LOUMIE'S ORANGE SLICE CAKE

2 sticks margarine	1 tsp baking soda
2 cups sugar	1 lb orange slice candy
4 eggs	1 small box dates
3½ cups plain flour	2 cups pecans
½ cup buttermilk	1 can coconut

Cream margarine and sugar. Add eggs one at a time. Dissolve soda in buttermilk and add alternately with flour. Cut orange slice candy and dates in small pieces. Roll nuts and dates and candy in small amounts of flour just to coat each piece. Add all ingredients and mix by hand. Bake at 250 degrees for 2½ hours. When cake is done leave in pan and pour glaze over top and let cool in pan.

Glaze: blend together well one cup orange juice and 2 cups powdered sugar.

CONNETTA'S REHEARSAL COCONUT PIE

2 cups sugar	⅔ cup buttermilk
4 eggs	2 tsp vanilla
1 stick margarine or butter	1 can coconut
	Unbaked pie shell

Mix all ingredients together and bake in unbaked pie shell at 325 degrees for 30 to 35 minutes. And that's about as long as Connetta's interest runs.

MARLENE'S HONEY PUMKIN PIE

1½ cups steamed canned
    pumpkin
¾ cup honey
¾ cup brown sugar
¼ tsp nutmeg
½ tsp salt

1 tsp cinnamon
½ tsp ginger
¼ tsp cloves
1½ cups evaporated milk
½ tsp vanilla

Mix ingredients in order given and bake in one crust. Sprinkle with nutmeg before baking. Bake at 425 degrees for 15 minutes, then 350 degrees for 45 minutes. Cool.

MAYBE MORE SQUASH CAKE

4 boiled squash (maybe
    more)
1 cup milk
3 cups sugar
1 tsp vanilla
2 eggs, scrambled up
    (but don't cook 'em)

1 block butter
3 cups flour (maybe
    more)
3 tsp baking powder (½
    tsp more for each
    extra ½ cup of flour)

Mix everything except flour and baking powder. Then add flour gradually. Maybe more, if you need it. Add baking powder (remember to add extra if you use more flour). Bake at 350 to 375 degrees for one hour.

FUNERALS,
WAKES,
AND CEMETERY
CLEANINS

ONE SIDE OF A CONVERSATION BETWEEN GRACIE DWIGGERS AND ROSETTA BUNCH ABOUT EDNA RAE'S WAKE AND FUNERAL, OVER THE PHONE

"Hello. . . . . Rosetta, that 'ew?. . . . . Yeah, it's Gracie here. Willard Lynn tol me you called. . . . . That's jus what I reckoned you was a callin about . . . . Yeah, Rosetta, I was so sorry you was outta town last week, durin it all. But, you can rest ashore I'm gone fill you in on the particulars. You boun ta heard a few of 'em, by now. . . . . Yeah, I figgered so. But, Rosetta, you wouldn'ta believed that wake a hers. . . . . Now, you stop me when I get ahead a myself. Can you hear me good? Cause, I want to start right at the beginnin, when she passed on, okay? . . . . Well, I was home and they called me to say it'od happened. Now, we was all kinely suspectin such a thing, but still, it jus like ta twisted me to pieces. . . . . Yeah. We was close as sisters. I loooved that Edna Rae. But I realized, quick as hot grease, I had to git a holt on myself. So I did. I thew all six a my young'uns in the backseat of that ol' jalopy a mine and headed dreckly over there, cause, I knowed full well, the famly'od be hungry and tired by the time they got back from the hospital, and all that torment. So, I got to Edna Rae's in about fifteen minutes of the time they called me. But, when I drove up, by the gas pumps in front a her store, I saw Reatha Faye, on foot, splittin them woods behind there, wide-Gawd-dawg-open. She had a apern on an it looked to me like it was filled with some kinda stuff, cause she had it all bundled up in the front like when you pick a mess a peas er sumpthin. At firse, I thought I's seein things. . . . . Yeah, it's plum snakey-lookin back there too. But, I'm absolutely positive, it was Reatha. I could tell er anywheres. . . . . Now, I didn't go through the store. I couldn't bare it, right yet. T'me that store WAS Edna Rae. So, I wen on round to the side and opened up the livin room door. Back behind there, where she lived with Flynt. Rosetta, I cain't remember whether you was here then, or not, but that's the same place she raised all them boys a hers 'fore she married him. . . . . Yeeees, that's right. They ain't a one of 'em that can stand 'im, neither. But that Edna

21

Rae, honey, shorered'n hell, liked 'im. I guess that's natural of 'em, uh? . . . . Well anyways, I wen on in to straighten things and cook 'em some supper. I's doin it, mainly, for Edna Rae and the boys, of course. An I got this, kinely like a . . . a . . . cole shiver on me. Like somethin was wrong. It was, as if, Edna Rae was tryin to tell me somethin. I could see that, as shore as I'ma talkin in this telephone. So, I eeeasied on in and started lookin aroun, when I foun there weren't nairy a pitcher left on that little whatnot stan she had sittin over in the corner. And, her bedroom was stripped, too. All the family pitchers was gone from er bureau. That Reatha Faye, had come in there while everybody was gone and just cleeeeaned house. . . . . She just raaaked 'em off with er arm, right in er apern, looks like to me, and took off out the backdoor. That's when I drove up and seen er goin. They ain't no way we can prove it, but you know, as well as I do, what she had bunched up in there, runnin thataway. . . . . Nooooo Rosetta, it weren't groceries. An the family album's gone, too. Can you b'lieve that. Edna Rae's close frien ramshackin er house, 'fore they could git er to the undertakers. Now them boys, won't have one pitcher of their Mumma. . . . . Ain't it! . . . . Ain't it! . . . . You right, Ro-setta. That's jus what she is, no matter how you spell it. She's gone git hers. But what really keeps a-naggin at me is, how on earth'od she find out Edna Rae'd died, right egsackly, when she did. . . . . Yeah. . . . . Yeah. You got it Rosetta, and I ain't had to put a word in yo mouth, neither. You hit it on the sof spot. He double-dawg didn't want the boys to have a one a them pitchers of er, outta pure meanness. They was in cahoots together. That's what they was. Heeee called er an tol er to do it. He's anuth-er'n whose gone git his, an you can pencil that in, too. I always did wunder bout 'em anyways. But Rosetta, you ain't heard nuthin yet! It gits thick as Miss Fayda Mae's gravy.". . . . .

Just about then, Willard Lynn's patience wore out and he couldn't listen to another word. So, he flipped up his Lazy Boy, as if he was driving it, and splurted out, "Gracie, you better git off that phone. They's five more on that party line might wanta use the thing." Gracie cupped her hand over the mouthpiece and snapped back, "Okay, Willard, don't you start. All they do is listen, anyway.

They don't ever tawk on the damn thing. All of 'em scareder'n biddy shit of it."

Without a pause her hand came off the receiver and she continued. "I'm sorry Rosetta, Willard was a houndin at me. He cain't stan it when I'm enjoyin myself. Anyways, I cooked supper for 'em an we tawked a bit. I was jus gittin ready to leave, when, a knock come on the door. I had a feelin who it was, since she's always the first one at every death. With her biiiig pot of perlow. An 'specially, if it's a widderer. . . . . Yesss, you rite. It was Naireen Sikes in the tightis clothes you ever witnessed. Ol Big Ruby Dukes calls er, right to er face, too, "Naireen The Perlow Queen, Tightest Clothes I'd Ever Seen." She don't miss a chance, that Ruby. But let's do credit to er. . . . . Now Rosetta, don't be ugly. Naireen's always there. And she ain't never failed at makin the best, damn perlow in these scrubs, maybe 'cept for poor ol' Edna Rae. Now, that must mean sumpthin, these kinds a times? . . . . But, Rosetta, you wouldn'ta believed it. Fore I could git the kids piled back in that car and git on, the food started a gatherin. That side porch was like a parade of Sunday dinners for about an hour. . . . . Well, first Naireen, then Jeweldeen Buck, ta'reckly here comes Big Ruby Dukes, and it wadn't long after that 'fore Lucille Collins showed up with her two boys a luggin a washtub. Thank Gawd, it didn't need to be put in the box. . . . . Yeah, it was cole drinks. But you see me, like I am, I was shore it had beer stuffed down under the ice. . . . . Of course it did. Tell me I don't know Lucille Collins, or my name ain't Gracie Dwiggers. Rosetta, I ain't never saw so much food. It jus kept a pourin in. You'da thunk the Pope 'ad died. . . . . Yeas. . . . . n while we on that, you know they ain't nuthin juicier n church gossip. An you was aware 'at Edna Rae was a converted Catholic, wadn't you? . . . . I thought so. . . . . Yeah honey, her first husband was and she wadn't and didn't join', neither. But when he died she raised them boys by the book. Edna Rae always said she took them vowels and she was gone keep'em. Yeeeears later, she went on down there and changed over. But, what went and stirred the water the wrong way was, when she married Flynt, against just about everybody's good advice, he was a divorced man. And you know what them Catholics think a that. . . . . They, flat out, wouldn't bury er in the church, cause of it. But, they said they'd send a pries to the cemetery. Can you imagine that. As I see it, the way she raised them boys and all, they shoulda honored er for that, even, if she'da done nothin else the rest of er life. Which, she, Gawd rest er soul, did plenty more. An uhnotherthing, honey, whether she did or hadn't did, whatever it is, they said she didn't do, ain't no reason to keep her from the Lawrd, if that's what she wanted. Ta me, as hoooly as them fellers might be, I ain't sayin one way er another, but, I'm tawkin, when it comes . . . right . . . down . . . to the gate, they ain't noway they cain git her in, and shorereden hell cain't keep her outta, heaven. But, Rosetta, at that gate's the only time where I can see it'd really matter. . . . . Oh, I'm sorry, Rosetta. I got own it again. . . . . Thank gawd Willard didn't hear me. . . . . Oh yeah, they did send one, Rosetta, but the poor thing was so old he didn't know whether HE was comin or goin, much less understan his english. But we overlooked all that, cause it was the most magnannygoshus day, ever. Edna Rae loved sayin that when the weather was good. . . . . Ain't it. . . . . Cause, you know, as well as I do, if Edna Rae hadn'ta been in that box she'da been on Saunders' Dock a-fishin, certainly not in church or at a funeral home. We alllll knew that. . . . . Rosetta, are you there?. . . . . Rosetta, you've done gone and let me git ahead a myself, after I asted you to stop me. Now, where was I? . . . . Oh yeah, thank you. The food was jus pooooourin in. I never seen so many different kinds of deviled eggs in my life. . . . . Yeah, everybody's hens had ta been a layin double. Well, I crammed it all in Edna Rae's icebox till I couldn't git another mouthful in it and I took the rest home. Cause I knew they'd need it later on. Now, I can tell you, they was some gooood food. . . . . it bein her wake and all. Everybody fixin for it knowed it was gone be helt up to Edna Rae's cookin standards. So, it had to be mouthwaterin. . . . . Like I was sayin, I packed the icebox, and strung it out all over the tables. Rosetta, there weren't a spare inch left. Well I tol 'em all goodnight. And I got outta there quick as I could, 'fore them tears started runnin'. . . . . It's that nighttime what gits you and makes it hardis' to hold on to yourself. But honey, if I'd had a inklin of what was to come, I'da took me a pill and not waked up till waaaaay on inta nex week. . . . . Just . . . hold . . . own . . . Rosetta. I got to catch myself. When I tell about it, I don' know whether to laugh or cry. But, knowin Edna Rae, as I did, I'm shore she'da done a little bit of both. Do you remember how, when somebody tol a joke, she useta cross er legs to keep from peein?. . . . . Oh yeah, she loooved them jokes. . . . . And was full of 'em too. Well, all I can do now is just hope and pray she'da laughed with us on what took place the nex' day. An I feel shore she woulda, after she got over the shock. . . . . But even, Edna Rae'd a had to tax er funny bone to git to that point. . . . . Well, I didn't go right over the next day but I did send two a my girls. They little but they can cleeean, honey. T'ward evenin Willard Lynn went and got the girls 'fore they brought Edna Rae on back home. Meanwhile, I dug down in my closet and foun my funeral frock, hat and shoes and put 'em on. Then I put on my face. No, Rosetta I wear the whitest powder I can find. After that I put on my eyes. A little rouge cake on my cheeks, so I don't look like I'm dyin, and no lipstick. . . . . Why-ay? It's too wicked lookin at a time like that. But I was dressed by the time they got back, so we headed straight on over there again, 'fore the people started coming. When I walked in, I couldn't b'lieve the food that'od showed up durin the day. And someone had gone to the church and borried foldin chairs and spreaded 'em all over the house. Down at the end of that looong livin room Edna Rae was laid out in her coffin. They was two big buckets of yard flowers on each end, somebody'd brought. And the two big floor lamps that them undertakers cain't have a funeral without. . . . . Yeah, they tol me one time them lights made it look 'other worldly'. I ain't shore I like that, specially if it means what ta hell I think it does. . . . . Yeah, you right Rosetta, it was Phillis Willis with that yard full of flowers she's got. It was real pretty. But I was itchy to git on and do my respecks 'fore anybody else got there. Private, like. So, I eased up, said a little prayer and talked to her. . . . . Yeah, just as natural as could be. . . . . Like, she was sleepin. So at peace. But they was sumpthin wrong. Sumpthin that bothered me . . . I think it must a been er hair . . . toooooo done up. Seems to me, they always over fix 'em. Well, I helt on to myself, that time, cause I knew I had to run the show. An I'm so glad I paid my visit when I did. . . . . Cause, just as the sun went down the people started arrivin in twos n threes. I swear to Jehovah, some of 'em was already goose-eyed when they got there. . . . . I don't know why, Rosetta, they haf to be all lickered-up to go somewhere. . . . . Like hell, it never'od work, Rosetta. That Lucille'd done set up a full-fledge bar on the back porch, where nobody that didn't want to, couldn't git seen. Then, on about black-dark, the house got crowded. All the women took over the inside, as usual, and was eatin house outta home. An empty chair wadn't to be foun. And the men had took to the yard, smokin, drinkin, tellin jokes and lord knows what all. But you can imagine, cain't you Rosetta. . . . . Yeah, Reatha Faye was there. Just spinnin an twirlin an a flittin like sumpthin sent from heaven. . . . . Nerve! . . . I never'od seen such a thing. Well, honey, they all got dawg drunk 'cept for the family, of course, and started mixin and minglin together. It was hard to keep the place lookin decent with all the cups, drinks and plates scattered ever-which-a way. But we tried. . . . . I was real proud of them boys, too. They was takin it real good. Flynt claims he got tired of it all, so he went and sit on their bed. Well, everybody, naturally, just followed 'im, 'specially Reatha Faye. . . . . No honey, Naireen was an angel. I watched after er like a hawk. She was the biggest help to me. . . . . Yeah, I tol you, you could depen on her. But Reatha had some outfit on that was as gauzy as it was gaudy. Looked like she was the one bein buried. An she placed herself, on the bed, right nex to Flynt. Now, I ain't judgin nobody for puttin their hand on anybody's knee, but I'll always wunder if it was the right time and place for Flynt to do that to Reatha Faye, even though, they was, all, close as pinfeathers and the bedroom was filled with people. However. . . . . Rosetta, I ain't Claudette Cahill and Chestine Butler. . . . . They was juiced-up to their gullets and didn't like what they seen one bit. . . . . No, Rosetta, they ain't no bloodkin. They just inlaws from waaaaay-back. . . . . Yeah, troublemakers. Well them-two went

into the awfulist cussin streak you'd ever heard come from anybody's mouth, not even ol Big Ruby Dukes coulda top 'em. An it
was aimed right at Reatha and Flynt. I knew what was comin nex,
and shore nough, Claudette grabbed Reatha Faye right by that
great big pone a teased-up hair and started pullin. Chestine latched
on to a handful of dress like a bulldog, just a-snatchin as hard as
she could. Everybody scattered, tumpin over everythin in sight. So,
I ran to the coffin, closed the lid and stood right by it. The tussle
finally ended up out in the yard. . . . . Yeah, you right
Rosetta. If you gonna fight . . . the yard is the place. But the thing
about the thing, thank Gawd, was the boys had already gone off
to spend the night, you can understan that, when it all broke
loose. . . . . Yeas, that was a blessin. So by now, they
was fallin, tumblin and pullin each other all over her flower beds,
till you couldn'ta tol who was fightin and who wadn't, if you'd
wanted to. An cars was diggin outta there like it had been raided.
Finely, Edna Rae's nephew, who's a debady sherff, ran to his car and
turned on the sighreen and flashin light and stopped the whole
thing in it's tracks. . . . . I had a feelin you'd wanta
know that. Well, she looked a mess . . . like she'd been put
through a wringer. As they always say, honey, the feathers was
pulled. But she didn't have a scratch on er. Now them other two
was scraped up one side and. . . . . yeah, they always
do more damage. . . . . cause they wind up fightin
each other. . . . . Honey, Claudette and Chestine will
paaay to fight. It don't matter who it is. They'd jump a Bush
Hawg. But I must say, Rosetta, and don't you repeat this, I was
secretly on their side. . . . . I know I ought to be
ashamed of myself but I ain't. . . . . Yeah . . . by then,
we was egghausted and just about everyone was gone. Them that
wasn't, all pitched in and cleaned the place. You cain't imagine . . .
Rosetta, that front yard of hers looked like the hawgs had got in an
wallered it down. . . . . Oh yeah. The funeral went
fine. You never seen a soberer bunch, not even in a Baptist church,
Rosetta. But, you know as well as I do, somebody had to go show
their behin that day, too. . . . . Yeass, right in front of
a five mile funeral, Big Ruby Dukes leaped out of the car she's a
ridin in and jumped on the back of the debady sherff's motorsickle

and, away she goes, on to the cemetery, clingin to the back of that thing with er dress justa flyin. But that's Ruby Dukes. . . . . Ain't that the truth, honey . . . they ain't no changin it. Rosetta, I got away from the wakenight and I wanted to tell you what I did. Then, I got to go, else, you know who'll be screamin again. As usual, me and Willard was the last to go home. But 'fore I did, I went back in there, lifted the lid and tol Edna Rae I was so sorry it'od hap'emed that way. But, you know Rosetta, she had this, kinely like, peaceful little smile on her face, it looked to me like. And I coulda sweared I heard er say, "Don't worry 'bout it, darlin, I been through a whole lot worser'd'en this.". . . . . Rosetta. . . . . are you cryin? I didn't mean to upset you, honey, but the truth is the truth. Now, I gotta go 'fore I git skint alive. Bye, bye honey. See you t'morrah. Oh! Wait a minute! Wait a minute. This ought to cheer you up a little bit. . . . . Yeas, honey, Reatha Faye brought them pitchers back. Said she was watchin 'em for Edna Rae and the boys. . . . . You don't think I know that, Rosetta. She got a taste a the Devil at the wake and got scared. . . . . She still looks a little be-shovelled to me. Bye . . . Bye, honey.

———————————

MISS FAYDA MAE'S FRUIT COCKTAIL GRAVY COBBLER

1 large can fruit cocktail	3 Tbs margarine
¼ cup light brown sugar	1 cup Bisquick or the
2 tsp cornstarch	likes
1 can Mandarin oranges	½ cup cream

With the syrup from the drained fruit, mix the light brown sugar and cornstarch. Stir over fire till thick. Add the fruit and bring to a boil. Empty into a square baking dish and smear on 2 tablespoons of the margarine. Mix Bisquick, cream and the rest of the margarine (it should be moist but stiff) then spoon over the hot fruit cocktail. In a 400-degree oven cook for 20 minutes. The biscuits should be golden.
Serves 6.

AUNT BIMMIE'S MEAT AND BEANS

2 lbs ham hocks with a lot of meat or chopped ham	½ cup diced celery
	2 Tbs ketchup
	1 tsp molasses
2 lbs dried big lima beans	1 tsp French's mustard
	1 tsp salt
6 cups water	Black pepper to taste
2 onions, chopped	

Pick your beans good. Put them in a big pot of water and bring to a rolling boil. Turn off the fire and let sit for one and a half hours. Add everything else, cover and slow cook for 2 hours. Take the meat off the bones. Cook a pot of rice and chop a fresh bowl of onions to go with them.
Serves 6.

ROSETTA'S SPANISH POTATO CROQUETTES

6 medium potatoes, boiled	1 Tbs minced onion
3 Tbs buttermilk	1 Tbs minced green pepper
1 Tbs margarine	1½ tsp salt
1 egg, beaten	¼ tsp pepper

Whip the potatoes and all the above together. Pour out into a 2 inch deep pan and chill. Then form into croquettes (like little 2 or 3 inch high pones).

4 cups saltine crumbs
3 eggs (slightly beaten)

Roll the croquettes in the crumbs, then in the eggs and back in the crumbs. Deep fry in fat till golden brown and done through (2 or 3 minutes). Put on paper to drain. Delicious cold.
Serves 6.

EGGS IN INDIAN GRAVY

9 hard-boiled eggs, chopped	3 cups sweet milk
8 Tbs chopped onions	½ cup water
5 Tbs margarine	2 tsp salt
4 Tbs flour	⅛ tsp pepper
7 tsp curry powder	3 cups of cooked rice

Cook the onions in the margarine. Take off the fire and stir in the flour and the curry powder. Put back on the fire and heat till smooth. Slowly pour on the milk and water while stirring until it thickens. Add eggs, salt and pepper. Pour over rice in casserole, cover and take it out the door cause there's hungry people waiting on you.
Serves 4.

DEVILED PECAN EGGS

8 hard-boiled eggs
1 tsp French's mustard
1 tsp grated onion
½ tsp salt

1 tsp vinegar
¼ cup mayonnaise
½ cup pecans, chopped

With a sharp knife, half the eggs long ways. Remove yellows and fork till mashed. Mix in all the other ingredients and stuff back in the eggs. Arrange on platter. Don't forget to tape your name to the bottom of the dish.

LUCILLE COLLINS' DEVILED FISH EGGS

8 hard-boiled eggs
4 Tbs margarine,
     softened
3 tsp of them little black
     fish eggs

2 tsp vinegar
1 tsp sugar
⅛ tsp black pepper

Cut eggs the long way. Take out yolks and mash with fork. Then mix with sugar, margarine, vinegar and black pepper until very smooth. Fold in the fish eggs and stuff the whites with the mixture. Sprinkle with paprika.

"She brings 'em cause they go good with beer," Gracie says.

GRACIE'S SUGAR COOKIES

2 cups sifted flour
1½ tsp baking powder
¼ tsp salt
4 tsp milk

1 egg
⅔ cup Crisco
¾ cup sugar
½ tsp vanilla

Sift together the dry things. Cut the sugar into the Crisco and add the vanilla. Beat in egg till fluffy. Add milk and stir till smooth. Slowly blend in the dry mixture. When creamy store in the icebox till chilled. Roll out on a floured spot until an eighth inch thick. Cut in circles and bake for 10 minutes at 350 degrees on an ungreased sheet. Remove from pan and cool.

Makes 22 to 26 cookies.

LEFTOVER COFFEE DESSERT

6½ cups very strong hot
coffee
3 packs Knox gelatin
½ cup cold water
2 sticks cinnamon
4 cloves

1 cup light brown sugar
1 tsp minced crystallized
ginger
¾ cup toasted chopped
Brazil nuts

Cook the coffee for 10 minutes on a slow fire with the cinnamon and the cloves in it. Fish out the cloves and the cinnamon. Soften the gelatin in the water. Add it and the sugar to the hot liquid and stir until it dissolves. Chill in the icebox. When it starts to set and thickens fold in the ginger and the Brazil nuts. Chill until very firm. Tear into hunks and place in a bowl with whipped cream. If you want, add a little Irish Mist to the cream.

CORN PUDDIN

2½ cups fresh cut corn kernels
2 eggs, beaten
1 cup milk
¼ cup finely chopped celery
¼ cup finely chopped onion
1 stick margarine
2 Tbs flour
1 tsp salt
½ cup Ritz cracker crumbs

With the margarine in a cast-iron skillet, cook the celery and the onions till soft. Blend the flour and the salt to the mixture. When it begins to bubble slowly pour in the milk, constantly stirring. While rapidly stirring, bring to a rolling boil and stir and cook for 2 or 3 minutes more. Add the cut corn and stir in the beaten eggs. Pour into a greased baking dish. Cover with Ritz cracker crumbs and cook in the oven at 350 degrees until firm or a toothpick comes out clean. Serves 6.

CHESTINE BUTLER'S MEAT LOAF

2 lbs ground meat
½ tsp salt
½ tsp black pepper
1 cup celery, chopped
2 Tbs Worcestershire sauce
1 can tomato soup
1 tsp baking powder
3 eggs, well beaten
1 onion, chopped
1 green pepper, chopped
2 cups hard bread, crumbled
½ cup ketchup

Work everything into the ground meat except the ketchup. You've got to use your hands. When blended, put in a greased glass baking dish and cover with the ketchup. Bake at 375 degrees for one hour being careful not to let it burn.

Chestine slices it and makes cold sandwiches with mayonnaise and mustard. Serves 6.

CLAUDETTE CAHILL'S BOILED AND BAKED HAM

Whole ham (pre-
   cooked)
1 cup brown sugar
2 Tbs French's mustard
6 cloves

Cold beer
Water
1 jar Maraschino
   cherries, cut in half

Cut off some of the fat. Crisscross ham, making diamond-shaped cuts. Boil in the sugar, mustard, cloves and enough beer and water to cover. When tender (an hour) drain. Put on baking pan and place cherries in all the diamonds. Then pour cherry juice over it and brown in the oven at 400 degrees for 15 or 20 minutes.

Claudette says, "You can take a ham anywhere."

REATHA FAYE'S SQUASH RITZ CASSEROLE

1 lb yellow squash, cut
   in rounds
½ cup crumbled Ritz (23)
1 onion, chopped
½ cup celery, chopped
   fine
½ cup grated sharp
   Cheddar cheese

¼ cup green pepper,
   chopped fine
2 eggs beaten
1 cup sweet milk
½ cup evaporated milk
¼ tsp salt
2 Tbs melted margarine
Pepper

Tenderize squash in a little bit of water, drain and mash. Mix all the other ingredients in with the squash. Butter a casserole and put the squash mixture in it. Bake at 350 degrees for 30 minutes or so. When done it should be kind of like a pudding.

Serves 6.

AUNT SUTIE'S COMFORT BANANA PUDDIN

First, The Scratch Puddin:

5 eggs	1 cup sugar
1½ cups sweet milk	1 Tbs flour
1 cup evaporated milk	Pinch or two of salt
1 Tbs vanilla	

If you ain't got one, rig up a double boiler by putting another pot inside a bigger pot with water in it and put it on the fire.

Pour the milk into the heated pot. Mix together and add, very slowly, the sugar, flour and the salt to the milk, stirring constantly. Don't stop stirring. Cook for about 20 minutes more after it has started to get thick. Reserve egg whites in a clean bowl, and in another bowl beat the yolks. Stir a spoonful or two of the pudding into the yolks and mix thoroughly. Then add it all to the pudding and stir up very good. Stir and cook for 5 more minutes, take off fire and fold in the vanilla. Now that's your scratch puddin.

Comfort Crust:

Vanilla wafers
7 ripe bananas, sliced in rounds

In a baking dish make a layer of wafers and a layer of bananas, then pour on a layer of the puddin. Keep doing this until all the puddin is gone, but remember you must wind up with a layer of puddin.

The Meringue:

5 egg whites
½ cup of sugar
1 pinch of cream of tartar

Beat whites till peaked. Then add the sugar, a little at the time, and beat until peaks curl over and hold. Spread the meringue over the pudding and put it in a 425-degree preheated oven for 6 or 7 minutes. Careful not to let it get too brown. By the time you get to the wake or wherever you're going it will be set up good. It's also very good chilled.

AUNT MELVILLE'S OKRA AND TOMATOES

1 lb okra, sliced
1 can tomatoes
Onions

Lots of hot stuff
(Tabasco sauce,
Worcestershire sauce,
peppers)

Tump it all together and simmer 2 or 3 hours.
This'll perk 'em up.

SUE ETHEL'S SAUSAGES AND BEANS

1 lb hot pork sausage,
loose
2 cans red kidney beans
2 cans stewed tomatoes
2 cups tomato juice
2 or 3 bay leaves
1 large onion, chopped
1½ tsp seasoned salt

½ tsp garlic salt
1 tsp chili powder
½ tsp thyme
¼ tsp black pepper
1 cup whole kernel corn
2 stalks celery, chopped
1 green pepper, chopped

Brown onions, sausage, celery, and green pepper. Add everything else, cover and simmer for one hour.

WILLARD LYNN'S LIMAS WITH A TWANG

3 cups cooked dried lima beans
½ can stewed tomatoes
¼ cup finely chopped onions
2 Tbs brown sugar

1 tsp vinegar
1 tsp Worcestershire sauce
1 tsp French's mustard
4 slices bacon

Put your beans in a 2-quart baking dish. Mix mustard, Worcestershire sauce, vinegar, tomatoes, brown sugar, onions and 2 slices of diced bacon. Put over beans. Cut bacon into four pieces and lay on top. Bake in a 375-degree oven for 45 minutes to an hour.
  Serves 4.

JEWELDEEN'S DEVILED-CRAB EGGS

12 hard-boiled eggs
½ cups mayonnaise
1 small can crab meat, drained and flaked

3 Tbs finely chopped onion
1 tsp French's mustard
  Salt and black pepper to taste

Lengthwise cut the eggs in half and remove the yolks. Mash them up and mix well with the mayo, onion, mustard, salt, and pepper. Stir in the flaked crab meat and then fill the eggs back up. Chill. Garnish eggs with a tiny sprig of parsley. Don't load it down if you're takin 'em to a wake.

MRS. TOOLER DOOLUS' OVEN SPAGHETTI

1 lb ground meat
2 green peppers, sliced
1 medium onion,
    chopped
2 Tbs vegetable oil (only
    if you need it)
2 eggs, beaten
2 cups corn kernels

1 can stewed crushed
    tomatoes
1 can ripe olives, no pits
    Salt and black pepper
    to taste
12 oz spaghetti, cooked
½ cup Ritz cracker
    crumbs
    Oleo

Fry the ground meat until brown. Add the green peppers, the onions and the oil (if you need it) and cook until limp. Take off the fire and add the eggs. Then the corn, tomatoes, and olive and mix well. Add to the spaghetti and pour into a big baking dish. Sprinkle on the cracker crumbs and pat with oleo. In a 375-degree oven, bake for 40 minutes.

"With a loaf of lite bread, this'll feed the multitudes," Mrs. Doolus said.

Serves 6.

HOMALENE'S SOMBRERO BEAN DISH

1 lb ground sausage
1 can tomato sauce
1 can Old El Paso
    Enchilada Sauce
2 green peppers,
    medium to hot

1 large can pintos
1 medium bag of Doritos
¾ cup white cheese,
    grated

In a deep skillet cook sausage until it crumbles up real good but not brown. Add everything to the skillet in layers. Reserve some corn chips and cheese for the top. In a 350-degree oven bake covered for 30 minutes. Uncover for the last 10 or until top is crispy and brown.

She says you can eat 'em with your hat on.

FELICIA BATTEN'S SWEET FRIED PIES

2 cups sifted self-rising
    flour
¼ tsp baking powder
1 tsp salt
2 Tbs Crisco

1 egg yolk
¼ cup sugar
½ cup evaporated milk
    Canned fruit (apples,
      peaches or pears)

Into the flour, baking powder and salt cut in the Crisco. Mix egg yolk, milk and sugar then add to the flour mixture. With a rolling pin roll out to a quarter inch on a floured surface. Cut in 4-inch squares. Spoon on a little bit of fruit, remembering that you are going to fold them point to point, so they'll come out like triangles. Fold over the fruit and seal the edges with a fork. Repeat till all dough is gone. Fry in a skillet with about an inch of very hot shortening until brown.

You have to watch the ladies with these. They go easily into their pocketbooks for later. Delicious with a glass of milk.

BILLIE RONDA'S FAMOUS BOURBON FRANKS

½ cup good bourbon
    whiskey
½ cup tomato ketchup

3 tsp dark brown sugar
1 lb frankfurters
    Toothpicks

Stir together bourbon, ketchup, and sugar in a pan set over low heat. Now put the heat up, but don't let it boil. Cut franks into bite-size pieces and add. Stir a bit, cover the pot, and let sit on the back of the stove overnight. Next day, when you've got folks coming, just heat it up again without it bubbling. Then you've got yourself something—just make sure you've got toothpicks and a load of napkins for the drips. Toothpick 'em. Put on tray and surround with saltines. Some at the wake will just want to nibble!

Enough for a crowd!

GRAMMA DORA'S FRIED CHICKEN

1 medium fryer, cut up
1 quart buttermilk
2 cups flour
1 Tbs baking powder

1 tsp paprika
Salt and pepper
3 cups Crisco

Pour the buttermilk over the chicken and soak for a few hours. Drain off the buttermilk. Pat chicken pieces into the flour, salt, pepper, baking powder, and paprika. Heat Crisco in deep iron skillet and fry. Turn frequently to get that crispy brown. Takes about 25 to 30 minutes.

BIG RUBY DUKES'S PEACHADILLIES

1 package fluffy white
   frosting mix
1 cup flour
⅓ cup cooking oil

1 cup peach preserves
¼ tsp cinnamon
1 cup finely chopped
   almonds

Prepare frosting mix as directed on the package. To half of the frosting mix, add flour and oil. Pat into bottom of a greased 13 x 9-inch pan. Bake at 350 degrees for 10 minutes. Spread with preserves. Fold cinnamon and almonds into the remaining frosting and spread over preserves. Bake 25 to 30 minutes longer or until topping is golden brown. Cool slightly. Cut into bars.
   Makes 36 bars.

NETTY BLOCK'S SALMON CROQUETTES

1 tall can salmon
4 tsp margarine or oleo
¼ cup all-purpose flour
½ cup evaporated milk
1 Tbs lemon juice
1 Tbs finely chopped
 onion

Salt and pepper to taste
1 cup fine crumbs
 (saltines crumbled)
1 beaten egg
2 Tbs sweet milk
1 package frozen green
 peas in white sauce

Drain off the juice from the salmon and save a half cup. Get rid of all the skin and bones while flaking the meat. Melt oleo and stir in the flour. To this add your salmon juice and milk. Cook until thick, stirring constantly. Add lemon juice, onion, salt and pepper. Mix in salmon and put in the icebox till cold. Form into 8 balls, roll in crumbs and make cones. Dip in beaten egg and milk then back in crumbs. Fry in deep hot fat till brown, 2 to 3 minutes. Drain on paper towels. Fix peas by package directions and top each croquette.

Serves 4.

CANDY SILCOX'S CONFETTI EGGS

6 hard-boiled eggs
2 tsp finely chopped
 toasted almonds
2 Tbs minced green
 pepper
1½ tsp minced pimiento
1 Tbs chopped ripe
 olives

3 Tbs Hellman's
 mayonnaise
1 tsp salt
1 tsp vinegar
¼ tsp black pepper
 Dash hot pepper sauce

Cut eggs in half long ways. Take out the yolks and mash with a fork. Mix everything with the yolks and stuff the eggs.

Because of the color these might not be appreciated at some wakes.

ANY OCCASION PIMIENTO CHEESE SANDWICHES

1 5½-oz can evaporated
    milk
½ lb processed American
    cheese, diced

1 3-oz can pimientos
¼ tsp salt

Combine milk and diced cheese in the top of a double boiler and heat until cheese melts. Drain pimientos and mash. Add to the melted cheese, along with salt.

Makes enough for 8 sandwiches. But cut 'em up in quarters and they go a long way.

YELLOW-EYED DEVILED EGGS

1 dozen fresh yard eggs
    (boiled)
2 tsp mustard
1 Tbs mayonnaise

2 tsp sweet pickle relish
1 tsp minced onions
   Salt and pepper
   Paprika

Slice eggs in half, reserve and mash yolks. Blend in the mustard and mayonnaise. Add pickle relish, onion, salt and pepper. Stuff the egg whites with the yolk mixture and lightly sprinkle with paprika.

NAIREEN THE PERLOW QUEEN'S SAUSAGE PERLOW

2 lbs smoked sausage
½ cup onion, chopped
¼ cup celery, chopped
2 Tbs bell pepper, chopped
1 piece garlic, chopped
1 regular can stewed tomatoes
1 tomato can of water

1 fist of thyme (the coarse kind)
3 bay leaves
2 hot green peppers or Tabasco to taste
Salt and black pepper
2 cups rice, Uncle Ben's
4 cups water

In a good heavy perlow pot, fry sausage, onions, celery, bell pepper and garlic till brown. Add tomatoes and the one can of water. Bring to boil, add thyme, bay leaves, hot pepper, salt and pepper to taste. Cook down for 20 to 25 minutes. Add rice and water and bring back up to a boil. Put tight lid on and simmer for 45 minutes, stirring once about half way through. If it's too soggy take the lid off for a while. If it's too dry add a bit more water.

"That Naireen is sumpthin. She's at the door with her pot, 'fore you can say perlow," Gracie said.

OVEN BROCCOLI

1 stick margarine
1 large onion, chopped
1 small can mushrooms
1 box frozen broccoli

8 oz cheese, chunked
1 can cream of mushroom soup
1 cup Uncle Ben's rice, raw

Fry onions in margarine till tender. Drain and add the mushrooms, then the broccoli, salt and pepper to taste. Cook until tender, about 15 minutes. Mix the cheese and mushroom soup together and add to what's already in the frying pan. Cook the rice in two and a half cups water, and add it. Pour it all into a casserole and bake for half an hour at 325 degrees or for 10 minutes in a microwave. Bread crumbs and Parmesan cheese may be put on top before baking.

LUCILLE COLLINS' WHISKEY PIE

Crust:
1½ cups graham crackers,
    crushed
¼ lb butter, melted
⅓ cup sugar
    Dash cinnamon

Filling:
12 oz cream cheese
½ cup sugar
2 eggs, beaten whole
1 Tbs flour
3 Tbs whiskey

Topping:
1 cup sour cream
3 Tbs sugar
1 Tbs whiskey

Make a kind of dough mixing all the crust ingredients together and press them into a pie pan, covering bottom and sides. Soften cream cheese, beat altogether with flour, sugar, eggs, and whiskey until thick as cream. Pour into the graham cracker shell. Bake at 375 degrees for 20 minutes. Mix the topping ingredients and spread on pie and bake 5 minutes more. Chill.

Lucille says, "This is strickly for wakes."

FAMILY REUNIONS,
BARBEQUES,
FISH FRYS,
AND PICNICS

POLLYS & MOLLYS

In Bacon County, Georgia, there's a town called Coffee. And in that town there's a chapter of the U. D. C. that, at one time, sported the largest number of surviving daughters of a Confederate soldier anywhere in the South, or, for that matter the world. The Captain Ovid Osteen Newberry Chapter of the United Daughters of the Confederacy had this organization sewn up on the local, state and national level. Now, they weren't moneyed (in fact, they were land-poor), but no one would have ever known it by the way some of them kept up the proud, proud front. There was Fannie Newberry Perry, Annie Newberry Walters Potter Floyd (Fannie said, "She keppa marryin 'um an they jus kept own a dyin"), Ovella Newberry Drake, Carrie Newberry Wooten, Molly Newberry Vanups, and Polly Newberry Vanups. The two youngest, Polly and Molly, married sophisticated Charleston railroad men and moved up and away in the world, never, again, to let on that their family didn't have two dimes to rub together. However, by rights, they did have the most money of all the girls, but it was, to no means, a fortune. They could afford to buy a fur, a fancy hat and a diamond. They both drove big, long black cars, too, especially, when they went to see their Bacon County country sisters.

Ovella said, "They jus tryin to keep up with them Charleston women who've got diamond rings big enough ta eat dinner on and more than ample blue rinse in their hair to color the Satilla River all the way to Woodbine." So, it seems, when you've come from a little country town and have lived in Charleston your entire married life with all those Van Dasterpoops, as Ovella calls them, you can't imagine how far down the road Coffee, Georgia must have seemed. Still, the only reason they had been accepted into Charleston society, at all, was because of their connection with the world's largest chapter of the U. D. C. in the South, even if it was in Bacon County, Georgia. And that was the ONLY reason. Now that was prestige to them Charleston folks. The sisters couldn't talk enough about their daddy, Ovid Newberry Newberry Newberry Newberry, otherwise they would have been considered South Georgia trash—

which they were from time to time. However, most of their children had heard it all too many times and couldn't wait to get back down in the swamps and scrubs of South Georgia and North Florida just to escape what they called "the Charleston Blue Bloods." The Newberry name had gotten Molly and Polly out of the woods and into town, but their children couldn't return to the swamps and scrubs fast enough.

Big Polly had a daughter and named her Molly Newberry Vanups. Big Molly had a daughter and named her Polly Newberry Vanups. Both of the daughters married brothers from a questionable Cracker family of the Georgia-Florida border area. Questionable by Charleston standards, anyway. So now, there was Floyd and Polly Newberry Vanups Bevels, Lloyd and Molly Newberry Vanups Bevels. And the two of them had had umpteen children, too, who were all just as ladened with names, like walking family trees. But Floyd and Lloyd ignored all of it. They didn't care who was named what. So, it was left, totally, up to the women to keep it going. And they did. Sometimes without catching a breath.

It was the six sisters, four of them that had populated ever dirt road in Bacon County and the two that had tried to get their toehold in Charleston society. They were ALL obsessed by the Newberry name. And as time went on Big Polly and Big Molly, after losing their husbands, started feeling the guilt of having neglected the Vanups's name. All they had ever thought about was the Newberrys, because it was their ticket. They had Newberryed their children up the wall and right under the noses of all those Charleston Vanupses, too. So now in their old age they wanted to do something about this neglect, while they still could. And it was such a perfect and convenient time to make amends. The Charleston Gazette had just run a big article on the Vanupses, letting everybody know from Savannah to Myrtle Beach that there was to be a big Vanups family gathering in the form of a barbeque, fish fry picnic. The paper requested the presence of everyone bearing the Vanups's name and anyone else directly related 'by blood' of course. The Gazette also advised the families to bring their own special covered dish to be shared on one big common table with everyone, but the barbeque and the fish would be furnished. It said it was to take place at the

Vanups State Park on Bunters Island right outside of Beaufort. Big Molly and Big Polly were thrilled about the coming event. They figured that it was their chance to uphold the Vanups's name and, after all these years, to redeem themselves, just a little bit. They believed, at their age, each one of these gatherings might be their last. So, they both sent out the article to all their children and made the decree that not only were they all expected to go to the reunion but they would also congregate at their respective mothers' homes (next door to each other) on Gardenia Lane and that they would all drive the sixty-some-odd miles from Charleston in a caravan, procession style. Both Big Molly and Big Polly feigned close to the grave illnesses to make sure Polly and Molly and their broods would come all the way from Florida.

On the day of the reunion, it was obvious from the sheer numbers that the decrees and faked sinking spells had worked to rally the family together one more time as only a Southern mumma can do. Both of the houses were filled with great-great-grandchildren right on up to the sons and daughters. And the cars were lined up on the street ready to begin the pilgrimage to the Vanups Family Reunion. When they had packed them with food of every description known to the South and equal numbers of children, all ages, the caravan slowly pulled out onto the highway. Big Molly and Big Polly in the first car, with one of their oldest sons driving and one riding shotgun, began to reminisce about their late husbands, Russ and Gus, as they passed through Rantowles, and about how Molly and Polly had been born while on a railroad expedition down into North Florida and how they've lived there ever since. While they passed Garden Corners, they talked about the christening when Big Molly stood for Big Polly's Molly and Big Polly stood for Big Molly's Polly. And that Molly and Polly were as devoted to each other as Polly and Molly had been down the years. Two sisters with two daughters, each as the other's namesake. This to them was the way to keep their families double-connected. However, not long ago at a Newberry Reunion, Ovella was ostracized after having said, "I bet you a crook to a dog's tail neither Big Polly or Big Molly, if you ask 'em point blank, couldn't tell you if they was married to Russ or Gus an whether it was Molly or Polly that's er daughter. I ain't even shore they know which 'un of 'ems which 'un, let alone, remember whether they was married to Floyd or Lloyd. They don't know Pollys from Mollys, anymore. It's a mess."

The chain of cars curled its way along the marshes into Beaufort and again the memories of Gus and Russ came pouring out. Or was it Russ and Gus. Then somewhere around Frogmore they both realized that, now, the reunion was scarcely over the bridge and waiting for them. They were just plain excited about the entire family making an appearance at the outing and thought not much else mattered to them, now. It was a time to show off all their family to whoever might have showed up from Charleston. And, after all, it had always been a numbers game with them.

As the car carrying Big Molly and Big Polly entered the gate of the park, they could vaguely see a slough of people up ahead. While fidgeting with their thick, thick glasses, and pushing and shaping their hair with a pat of the hand and a pick of the finger, they readied themselves for whatever was to come, knowing that their near blindness could be pulled out of the hat, and used, if it got to the point of not recognizing or remembering. When the Russ and Gus Vanupses' caravan was in full view of the crowd, every head under the big pavilion shed turned. Just as every eye in the procession focused in on, what looked every bit like, two separate reunions. One at each end of the large covered picnic area. This was obvious even to Molly and Polly, though they claimed seeing nothing else. They figured that it must be two different church groups having their own service to begin the reunion. At this point no one had ever owned up to the truth that the Charleston Vanupses were split in more ways than religious ones. And this publicly announced gathering was the end all at providing them with a reunion most would never recover from. Molly and Polly included.

Big Molly and Big Polly worked their way over with the help of the sons to the first crowd of people they could get to and began introducing and asking how each one belonged. They were straining ever so hard to see and recognize what they could. But not being able to see much and hearing even less, the sisters just started in. "Dahlin, how good to see you. Ouuh, you got that jet black hair just like my Polly." "Oh I haven't seen you in years, but that voice. It sounds just like Gus's Mumma." "Dahlin, look at you.

You got a tan as dark as my Molly. How's yo Mumma?" "I'd recognize you anywhere with that big toothy smile. You've got to belong to Vic and Clarice's bunch." "Them eyes, honey, you look just like Gus's daddy. There's no hidin that." The lack of response from the group didn't faze them as they went on and on, but the rest of the family stuck close to their cars in shock, not believing what they were seeing and, even less, what Big Molly and Big Polly were saying and doing. They resisted every attempt by the sons to guide them away from that crowd to the other end of the pavilion and went on greeting, kissing and recognizing. Little Molly and Little Polly refused to get out of the car and, even more, refused to put their food on that common table. And it was obvious now that there were two common tables in the making.

Big Molly and Big Polly's families had started trickling down to the other end of the shed and the place was buzzing. One of the uppity, old-line Vanupses, took it on herself, that she would go and get the "two old Jawga sisters," before they disgraced the family beyond repair, and, especially, before the newspaper reporter got there to take pictures of the picnic, even if she had to drag them back by the hair of the head. But she simply told them that it was communion time and she knew they didn't want to miss that. They recognized her, for real, and followed her like sheeps to the other end, just in time for the passing of the communion wafer by the priest. Kneeling, they took the wafer and said Amen. Then came the deacon with the wine chalice. Big Molly and Big Polly started fumbling in their pocketbooks for something. At the very same time they both came out with a fist full of pennies, nickels, dimes and quarters and dumped them right in the communion wine. While everyone bit their tongues, the priest and the deacon, completely bewildered, fished out (pocketed) the money and continued the rounds.

After the service the sisters were told of the mixup in the reunion and that they had been down at the other end, hugging and kissing a bunch of Negroes who happened to have the same last name and showed up for the wrong reunion. Simultaneously Big Molly and Big Polly gasped, "Ooooh, go own now!!" Their daughters jumped on them for disgracing their family in front of all those Charleston relatives. And the relatives were just as upset and had begun to lash out at them with their big Charleston mouths. But it hit Big Molly wrong. Her mind had slowed, but by no means was it gone, and like an old rusty Bacon County 'bobwire' fence that had been stretched and pulled for fifty years, it snapped. She took Big Polly's hand, clasped it and began in a loud, but dignified, voice, "First of all, I don't know what the hell y'all are so upset about, they everyone lighter than the whole bunch of you. And I distinkly remember hearing your granddaddy say, years ago, 'You may not like all the Vanupses but you GOT to love 'em. Defend 'em to the death.' So I think you all better sit down and have some of this food that everybody's brought and have a real good communion. And if that ain't enough, I got to tell you that even with these feeble ol eyes, I cain see they all look just like you."

She unclasped Polly's hand and said to her, low-like, "Now I don't nesairly believe in all this, but we cain't ack like animals. We just got to make the best of the sitchiation." Big Polly was quick to give her support and said, "Let's grab a plate and get to THEIR table for some good food. I'm thirty-years tired of Anna Belle Vanups's fancy Charleston Turnip Souffle. This'll almost be like goin home to Coffee." Big Molly said, "Lawd, I hope to Gawd the United Daughters don't get wind of this."

BIG MOLLY'S CHERRY COBBLER

4 cups canned pie
   cherries (No pits!)
¼ cups quick tapioca
1 pinch of ground cloves
¼ tsp cinnamon
1 pinch of salt

1 cup of light brown
   sugar
1 Tbs of grated orange
   rind
2 cups of Bisquick

In a great big pan mix the dry stuff (but not the Bisquick) and stir together with the pie cherries. Bring it up to a boil and cook for five minutes. Oleo down a two-quart baking dish and pour the cooked mixture in it. Make your Bisquick like it says on the box and spoon it on top of the cherries. Put it in the oven at 400 degrees for 20 to 25 minutes. Until the Bisquick is good and brown.

Serves 4 or more.

PICNIC TARTAR SAUCE

1 cup Hellmann's
   mayonnaise
¼ cup dill pickle relish

1 tsp grated onion
1 Tbs chopped canned
   pimiento

Stir together and put in the icebox to chill or take the stuff and make it when you get there.

Makes a bit more than a cup.

UNCLE BUBBA'S BARBEQUED RIBS

5 lbs meaty spareribs	1 tsp vinegar
½ cup ketchup	2 squirts of Tabasco
1 tsp brown sugar	2 Tbs French's mustard
1 tsp Worcestershire sauce	Salt and black pepper to taste

Grill the ribs over medium hot coals (hickory chips) until tender (two hours or so). Make sure you turn them a lot so as they don't burn. Mix up all your sauce ingredients and heat it so it will blend together. When the ribs are done spread the sauce over them and continue cooking for 20 or 25 minutes more. You can also bake them in a 300-degree oven for one and a half hours or until ribs are tender. Don't forget to turn the ribs once so they'll brown on both sides. Brush with the barbeque sauce as they bake.

Serves 6.

REUNION RICE PUDDIN

1 can crushed pineapple	1 Tbs lemon juice
2 Tbs white sugar	1 banana, chopped
1 cup quick cook rice	1 medium bag miniature marshmallows
1 cup water	
½ tsp salt	1 cup whipping cream, whipped

In a saucepan mix up the rice, water, syrup (from the drained pineapple), sugar and salt, and stir enough to moisten the rice. Cook to a quick boil, turn down heat, cover, and simmer 5 minutes. Set off the heat and let stand for 5 minutes. Now pour in the lemon juice, pineapple, banana, and marshmallows. Let it cool and fold in the whipped cream and eat.

Will serve 8, but better for 4.

SASSY'S HUMMINGBIRD CAKE

3 cups all-purpose flour	1 8-oz can crushed
2 cups sugar	pineapple, undrained
1 tsp salt	1½ tsp vanilla
1 tsp cinnamon	¾ cup chopped pecans
1 tsp baking soda	¼ cup black walnuts
1¼ cups cooking oil	⅔ cup mashed bananas
3 eggs, well beaten	

Combine all the dry ingredients in a large bowl. Add eggs and oil and stir until ingredients are moistened. *Do not use electric mixer.* Stir in vanilla, pineapple, nuts, and bananas. Spoon batter into three 9-inch round cake pans that have been well greased and floured. Bake for 25 to 30 minutes at 350 degrees. Cool 10 minutes, then turn out on cake rack to cool completely. Then frost.

Hummingbird Frosting: cream together two 8-oz packages of cream cheese and one cup softened butter. Blend in two 16-oz packages confectioners sugar. Add two teaspoons vanilla and one cup chopped pecans and mix thoroughly.

It's so sweet you can feed an army of hummingbirds.

OVELLA'S BEEFED-UP PORK AND BEANS

1 lb hamburger	⅓ cup brown sugar
1 large onion, cut up	3 Tbs French's mustard
1 quart can of any pork and beans	Bacon, enough to cover top
1 can tomato soup	Salt and pepper to taste

In a deep cast iron skillet brown the hamburger and the onion. Then drain off the grease and the juice. Add everything else to it and put the bacon on top. It'll take one hour in a 350-degree oven and it's ready.

Serves 6.

POLLY'S BEDEVILED CRABS

2 cups of fresh crab meat
(canned will do)
8 Tbs margarine or
butter
1 Tbs flour
1 Tbs lemon juice, fresh
squeezed
1 Tbs French's mustard
2 Tbs ketchup
2 tsp Worcestershire
sauce

1 dash of red hot sauce
1 pinch of dill
½ tsp salt
1 cup buttermilk
1 little sweet bell
pepper, chopped fine
1 little onion, chopped
fine
3 hard-boiled eggs,
chopped
½ cup bread crumbs

In a saucepan melt 4 tablespoons of margarine and slowly add flour, stirring till smooth. Put in the next seven things and pour on the milk, slow like, and cook over low fire till thick. Put a cover on it and set it aside. In a skillet fry the onion and pepper in about a spoon more of the margarine until they are soft. Combine with sauce and then add the egg and the crab meat. Press into tinfoil crab shells and pat on the buttered bread crumbs (buttered with the rest of the margarine). Bake in a hot 425-degree oven for 10 minutes. Make sure they are good and golden on the top.

Serves 6.

POLLY'S PUPPY HUSH-UPS

1¾ cups self-rising corn-
meal
1¼ cups buttermilk
1 small onion, chopped

1 egg
1 tsp salt
2 tsp sugar
8 Tbs drippings

Mix up the meal, sugar, and salt. Add the buttermilk and the beaten egg and stir till just right. Combine with onion. Heat up the drippings until they sizzle and crack, then add to the batter and stir fast. Plop by tablespoons in hot fat and fry till crispy brown. You might have to turn them if your fat is not deep enough. Don't overload the frying pan. When done, drain on paper.

Serve with fried fish, grits and cole slaw.

Will make 20 to 25 hush-ups.

EDNA MAE'S SLAWDOWN COLE SLAW

1 head cabbage	Some salt
Some sugar	Sweet pickle juice

Shred cabbage. Sprinkle sugar and salt onto cabbage and squeeze into cabbage with your fingers. Slaw should "weep". Add sweet pickle juice, seeds and all.

Sometimes you might have to turn your head so it'll cry.

HUMBLE LOG CABBAGE STEW

1 lb ground beef	1 16-oz can kidney beans
1 onion, sliced thin	1 cup canned tomatoes
1 cup cabbage, shredded	1 tsp salt
½ cup celery, diced	Dash pepper

Brown up the beef, then throw in the onions, cabbage, and celery. Cook until yellowish, then add two cups water and simmer for around 15 minutes. Slip in the rest of the ingredients and continue cooking for 15 to 20 minutes. And to give Mrs. Lincoln's stew a continental look, serve it on top of mashed potatoes. The two cups water may not be necessary, as there is plenty of juice in the canned beans and tomatoes.

AUNT BELLE'S CHARLESTON PEANUT BUTTER LOGS

1 cup crunchy style peanut butter 1 cup powdered sugar	3 Tbs soft butter 2 cups Rice Krispies

Mix all these ingredients together and roll into small logs. Dip in frosting.

Frosting:
1 cup powdered sugar
3 tsp milk
Vanilla

After dipping in frosting, roll logs in melted chocolate, graham cracker crumbs, or coconut. Set in a cool place, if they last that long.

FREDDIE LOU'S GEECHEED CABBAGE

4 slices bacon, cut up
⅓ cup finely chopped bell
   peppers
4 Tbs onions, chopped
1 can stewed tomatoes
1 tsp sugar
	1 tsp salt
	1 tsp French's mustard
	Dash of pepper sauce
	6 cups chopped cabbage,
	   cooked

In a big heavy pot fry bacon, green peppers, and onion until crisp. Add everything else and stir in good. Cook until heated through. Put on rice for the best and only way to get Geechee flavor.
   Makes 4 to 6 servings.

AUNT CALIOPE'S MIXED-UP BEANS

12 slices of bacon, cut in
    squares
1 medium onion,
    chopped
1 lb of chopped ham
½ cup dark brown sugar
½ cup ketchup
2 tsp French's mustard

1 tsp salt
1 can baby green limas,
    drained
1 can Boston style baked
    beans
1 can red kidneys,
    drained

Fry and drain bacon in skillet. Brown onion in drippings and take out. Pour out drippings and brown ham. Drain off fat. Mix all else together and put in a three-quart baking tin or dish, cover and cook in slow oven (300 degrees) about an hour.

Makes 6 to 8 servings.

GRANNY'S REVISED TEA CAKES

2 sticks butter (soft but
    not melted)
2 eggs

1 cup white sugar
4 cups self-rising flour
1 tsp vanilla

Cream the sugar and butter. Beat the eggs and add to the butter-sugar stuff. Mix thoroughly and pour on the vanilla. Sift the flour and combine with other. Mix well. Chill dough in the icebox until it is firm and you can roll it out. Roll it thin and cut to desired shapes. Bake in a 350-degree oven until golden on the top.

Makes about 4 dozen cookies.

MRS STAFFORD'S CAROLINA POUND CAKE

2 sticks butter	1 Tbs lemon
½ cup Crisco	1 tsp vanilla
3¾ cups flour	3 cups sugar
1 cup milk	1 tsp salt
5 eggs	

Cream together the butter and Crisco and sugar. Add milk and blend. Add eggs one at a time alternating with about a cup of the flour at a time, beating after each addition. Add salt. Add the lemon and the vanilla and blend. Bake in tube pan at 350 degrees for one hour and 15 minutes.

WAVY FLAG CAKE

1 package white cake mix	4 eggs
1 13-oz package strawberry gelatin	½ cup water
	¾ cup oil
2 Tbs flour	1 10-oz box frozen sliced strawberries

Mix cake mix, gelatin, flour, eggs and water. Beat at medium speed for two minutes. Add thawed strawberries, including syrup to the batter and beat one minute. Add the oil and beat one more minute. Pour into greased 13 × 9 inch pan and bake at 350 degrees for 40 minutes. Cool 10 minutes, then turn out onto platter. Frost.

Frosting:

1 cup whipping cream, beaten until stiff	Fresh blueberries
¼ cups powdered sugar	Fresh strawberries

Mix whipping cream and powdered sugar and frost cake. Stick the upper left hand corner with 50 blueberries and arrange fresh strawberries in stripes, against strips of cream between. Refrigerate.

KATHERINE BELLE'S APPLE CAKE

1½ cups cooking oil
2 cups sugar
3 well beaten eggs
3 cups raw, peeled, and
    diced apples

1 cup chopped pecans
3 cups flour
1 tsp soda
2 tsp vanilla

Combine the oil, sugar, eggs, apples and pecans in a large bowl. In a separate bowl sift the flour and soda. Add this to the apple mixture. Stir well with two teaspoons vanilla. Bake cake in 3 large layer pans at 325 degrees about 35 minutes.

Frosting/filling:
1½ sticks oleo
1 box light brown sugar
⅔ cup canned condensed
    milk

2 tsp vanilla
Grated coconut

Cook oleo, brown sugar, and condensed milk altogether over low heat. Let it come to full boil. Beat till cool, not cold, adding vanilla. Spread and sprinkle coconut between layers and on top.

ANNA BELLE'S FUDGE PIE

2 squares of bitter
    chocolate
1 stick of butter
2 eggs

1 cup sugar
1 cup flour
1 tsp vanilla

Melt chocolate and butter, add vanilla. Mix flour and sugar. Beat eggs and combine with flour mixture. Add chocolate mixture and mix well. Pour into a well greased pie pan. Bake at 350 degrees for 30 to 40 minutes. Will cut like a pie. Serve with whipped cream or ice cream. You double this recipe for a bigger pie.

GRANDMA'S POUND CAKE

2½ cups sifted self-rising
    flour
1½ cups sugar
¾ cups milk

1 cup shortening
½ cup butter
5 fresh yard eggs
1 tsp vanilla

Beat mixture for 20 minutes. Bake 350 degrees for one hour.
You won't believe the difference them fresh eggs'll give you.

BIG POLLY'S CRACKER CAKE

32 saltine crackers
2 cups sugar
1½ tsp baking powder
2 cups pecans
6 egg whites
1 tsp cream of tartar

1 8-oz carton Cool Whip
1 8-oz can crushed
    pineapple, well
    drained
Frozen grated coconut
Candied cherries

Use a rolling pin to crush the crackers until very fine. Mix them together with one cup of the sugar, the baking powder and pecans. Beat the egg whites until soft peaks form, add cream of tartar and the rest of the sugar and continue beating until stiff. Fold the mixture of dry ingredients into the egg whites. Pour into a well greased pan and bake at 350 degrees for 25 minutes or until golden brown. Watch closely. Remove cake carefully from pan after cooling. Chill. Frost with Cool Whip. Spread top with pineapple and cover with coconut, then garnish with cherries. The cherries are for when you need something extra fancy. Or you can frost it with Seven Minute Frosting and garnish with just cherries and pecan halves.

SEVEN MINUTE FROSTING

2 egg whites	⅓ cup water
1½ cup sugar	Dash salt
1½ tsp light corn syrup or	1 tsp vanilla flavoring
¼ tsp cream of tartar	

Place all ingredients except vanilla flavoring in double boiler. Mix thoroughly. Cook over water beating constantly with rotary or electric beater until mixture forms peaks, about 7 minutes. Remove from heat. Add flavoring. Beat until spreading consistency.

BIG MOLLY'S CRACKER PIE

3 eggs	12 saltines
1 cup sugar	12 dates
1 tsp baking powder	¾ cup pecans

Beat eggs. Add sugar and baking powder. Crumble saltines into this. Let stand. Cut up dates and add. Add pecans. Pour into buttered pie pan. Bake 350 degrees for 35 minutes. Serve plain or with whipped cream.

AUNT FANNY'S FISHFRIED OYSTERS

1 quart of big fresh
    shucked oysters (no
    coon oysters for this),
    drained
2 eggs, beaten

¼ cup Pet evaporated
    milk
    Salt and black pepper
1½ cups of cracker meal
    (crumble saltines real
    fine if you can't find
    cracker meal)

With a fork beat the eggs, milk, salt and pepper together. Drag each oyster through the batter then turn it in the cracker meal till it's covered. When you've got enough, put them in hot grease one at a time. Fry three minutes or until golden. Don't overcook your oysters. If they are small you can stick two or three together with the batter and then roll in the meal. You can also take this right to the picnic ground and fry them there.

Serves 6.

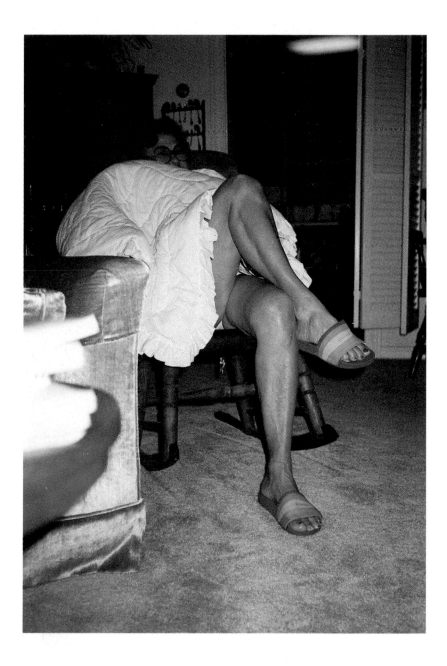

HOLIDAYS
AND
SUCH

CHRISTMAS SHOPPIN

Jerry Dale Holly was sowgded down in an old front porch rocker, mesmerized by the shooshing of a mile of pine trees that surrounded the house. In chilly weather the porch belonged to him and he used it to do his thinking, especially, while he made out his gift list for the coming Holidays. However, when Jerry Dale was younger he hid up-under the porch, listened to the grown-ups go on and on about everybody's presents, caught flicked cigarette butts to make smoking chimneys on little sand houses for Sanny Claws to come down, and chummed up doodle bugs out of their caniving holes for Juanita's main Christmas present. He was positive, his older sister by two years, just loved doodle bugs. Certainly, she always screamed loud enough.

Now, at thirteen, the rocker in a state of dilapidation is his place to chum and conjure a whole headful of catalogues, fancy department stores and wish books for his mind to go shopping in. He sits for hours. Stupefied. And for hours Mumma, Glennie Nell, hollers, "Jerry Daaaale. . . . . Jerry Daaaale. Me and yer sister cain't do all this Christmas cookin by areselves. Git . . . in . . . here, else you ain't gone git a mouth of it when it's done." Next time she'd holler, "Jerry Daaaale. . . . . Jerry Daaaale. . . . . git in here 'fore I slap you right off that front porch all the way to Biloxi." "Jerry Dale ain't heard nothin, Mumma. He's too busy shoppin for Christmas presents," Juanita said. "In his mine, you mean," Mumma snipped. But Jerry was deep, deep in thought, on what he could buy for Juanita now that she'd lost her taste for doodle bugs.

While Glennie Nell cooked, she seemed to harp continuously, in her head, at Jerald Dale Sr. about how she believed that Juanita was titched, at least Christmaswise, by them doodle bug presents. Because now, she wanted the craziest damn things every year. The kids could see her lips moving, to herself, as she went on reminding him, still in her head, of course, that at thirteen, Juanita asked for a statchers head of somebody named Bay Toe Vin, and last year she wanted a packige of some things called Papa Domes "cause they jump up outta the grease at ya when you try n fry 'em." That youn'un, what in the name o gawd will she wont nex? Mumma thought. She had already got a feeling, and she told Jerald Dale Sr. too, that, whatever it was, channel thirteen on the TV set was just as to blame for her lack of good sense as was Jerry Dale's doodle bugs. At least, when it come to choosing Christmas presents. Just recently she, couldn't stand it any longer and had to confess to one of her social club members, "We cain't git her out of that ol Chinese housecoat that she found in a box of things Jerald Dale brought back home from the War."

Jerry Dale used his big ears, each year, to be the first to find out what Juanita wanted. So, with his one or two trips to town at the most, he'd desperately try to find it himself. Then, if he couldn't, he'd tell his mother and father, just to watch them roll their eyes. But he was always set off by Juanita's pick and spent about all of his time and money trying to find it. Especially, since the sum-total he ever bought his Mumma was, Evening in Paris, talcum powder, or a lace handkerchief with a big GNH on it. She claimed that's all she ever wanted. His daddy was even less exciting to buy for; shaving foam, or Old Spice.

Juanita had decided long ago what she wanted, but so far she didn't let on to a soul. Not even Jerry Dale. But now might be the time to tell him and get him in off that front porch before Mumma's threats become real, she thought. She knew Jerry Dale would scramble for the kitchen at just one mention of the word present. So, it was her thinking that if she'd let them both know now, what she wanted for Christmas, it might also save Jerry Dale a trip, right off that front porch, to Biloxi.

Jerry Dale flew into the kitchen and paused at the edge of the table which he gripped with his fingers. Mumma folded her arms, tilted her head and looked over her glasses at Juanita. "Y'all wont laugh at me, will ya?" Juanita begged. Mumma said, "Honey, I might cry, but I'll never laugh at what YOU want for Christmas." Jerry Dale stood still and silent with his ears tweeked. As quick as her lips could get it out Juanita blurted, "Madame Butterfly." Jerry Dale didn't change a hair, but, with the queerest look, of absolute flabbergastation the child had ever seen, Mumma eyeballed Juanita and said, "Madum Budder Whooooo?" "Madame Butterfly," Juanita repeated. Mumma went back to stirring the cake batter, squenched up her nose real bad, and said, "Now . . . jis . . . whut, own the back of white cat's ass, is that?" Jerry Dale gripped the table even tighter, hoping Juanita would come up with a good explanation. Juanita began, "It's stowry-music." "Why who sings it, honey," Mumma, trying to keep calm, fished, "Dolly Parton? An if she didn't, I betcha she wrote it." "No, Mumma, it comes from a long time ago in It'ly. A man by the name of P-U-C-C-I-N-I wrote it," Juanita pleaded. "Well, I cain't even say that, let alone know what the hell kinda stowry is it. Nex thing ya know we gone need a interpruhtater ta tawk t' ya," she said with her over-worked nerves. "Weeeeell, it's about love," Juanita said. "Love! I mighten ta knew it," Mumma said with more irritation than ever, "I bet it's jis full a necked people, ain't it?" "Naooooo, it don't have necked people in it, it ain't that kinda love," Juanita said now, with a little more nerve of her own. But she quickly decided to get on and tell the whole story, while she could.

"It's about a soldier, looooongtime ago, that falls in love with one of them Japanese women and marries er while he was stationed over there. But he gits sent home and has ta leave er. He swears to er he'll be back as soon as he can." Mumma can't stand it and breaks in, "I've heard all that before." "Now, Mumma, let me finish 'fore you say another thing," Juanita, trying not to lose her place, picks up again, "But, you wrong, cause he does come back. Only thing is he brings an American wife with im." "I coulda told you that too, honey," Mumma assures her. Juanita tries to ignore her and goes on, "But the Japanese woman is so hurt n upset by it all till she commits suicide.". . . . . "That's it!! That's damnedest song I ever heard of. She oughten to a shot that son-of-a-bitch right in it. I tell ya, sometimes, I swear they all alike. . . . . But, honey, them mixed things jis ain't never worked, any ways. That's proof-puddin. Even, that ol Italian knew it." "Oh Mumma," Juanita shrugs, "that's not what the stowry means. It's a sad, sad romance that ends even sadder. . . . . "Ta Je-e-sus Cramminy!! And you want that for Christmas?" Mumma gripes. "Yes I do! It's the music that makes it so pretty," Juanita rested. Mumma said, "Huuuh!!"

Jerry Dale had hung to every word that his ears heard and had already, at least mentally, gone shopping. He knew his only hope was the local record store. If they didn't have such a thing, Mrs. Rachel might could order it for him, even if it took every penny he had. Mumma would go on and git Juanita whatever she wanted to anyway and he knew it wouldn't be "Madame Butterfly".

It took Mumma a good three weeks, with the help of the children, to stir and bake and cook-up one of her fine Christmas dinners. And each year when she started worrying, out loud, about cooking too much food, tight mouthed Jerald Dale Sr. would up and say, "Don't worry bout it, Mumma. It'll get et." She knew that he was right, and said to herself, "Them ciddy relatives 'od descend on 'em like Japanese grasshoppers and eat like they ain't et since last year."

Well, Christmas day came and Juanita got her "Madame Butterfly" and everyone else got just what they wanted too. Juanita went straight over to the record player and put it on. It was Christmas, Mumma couldn't say a thing. But she couldn't stand it either, so, she finished putting the touches on her dinner and took to the yard. She did love seeing the city relatives each Christmas, even though she felt a slight bit taken advantage of, but she figured, it was Christmas, and she did love doing it.

They all arrived about an hour later. Three carloads. Mumma was sitting on the front steps, Jerry Dale was in one rocker and Jerald Dale Sr. was in the other. When the crowd, stacked with presents, reached Mumma, she stood up to greet them, shy like. Greetings was always so awkward, she thought. Then, someone missed Juanita and asked where she was? They could hear the opera playing in the background but couldn't figure it out. They had never heard such a thing as that in Glennie's house before. Then, Mumma throws up her hands and said, "She's in there listenin to Pooch-er-Neen-Neenie er somebody." That broke more than just the ice that year. They all laughed, even Mumma, and went on in the house for a good Christmas Dinner. As they sat down, Madame Butterfly was over in the corner dying. The usually silent Jerald Dale Sr. again spoke up, "Gaw-od dawg! Somebody give that calf some more rope." "Cramminy ta Jesus, Jerald Dale Holly Sr., not right here at the Christmas table," Mumma said, putting a quieatous on the whole thing.

GLENNIE'S GUINEA HEN BAKED

2 or more cleaned
  guineas
  Small slab of salt meat
8 or 9 slices of smoked bacon
1 cup of strong coffee
½ tsp of vinegar

1 tsp of sugar
  Salt and pepper
3 rutabagas, cut in
  hunks
  Butter, salt and pepper
  to taste

First thing: boil rutabagas until tender. Add butter, salt and pepper and set on the back burner.

Guineas: first off, guineas are hard to come by. Most likely you got to raise 'em or know someone that does. But if you can git 'em they worth every bite. A grown hen'll weigh two and a half to three pounds cleaned. So you can plan on 3 to 4 people to the guinea. Course if you got other things, like I always do, it'll go a longer ways. I fix two or three to please my Christmas crowd. It's dark meat an has a light gamey taste to it. That's what makes it different from chicken. In fact, I clean it just like a chicken. Then I stuff a piece of salt meat and some black pepper in the hole. Wrap it all up with the slices of bacon and tie it up with string, if you want. Stick 'em in a fry pan or Dutch oven just big enough to hold 'em and a little deep so you don't lose your juice. It's best if your oven is already at 350 degrees or maybe a little hotter and they'll be done in an hour give or take a few minutes. But if you want to brown the breast take off the bacon and put it back in the oven for another 10 or so minutes. When it's ready, cut up the meat on a hot platter, surround with rutabaga hunks and keep it warm. From the juice spoon out some of the excess fat. Put in the coffee, sugar and vinegar. Move pot to a high burner and cook till all the guinea goody is loose from the bottom and sides. Pour this, hot, over the cut up meat and rutabagas. Take it straight to the table.

Careful of them old guineas cause you can cook 'em all day and still cain't bite into 'em.

GLENNIE NELL'S ROAST CHRISTMAS POSSUM

1 live possum	5 or 6 slices of bacon
½ cup vinegar	Salt and pepper
Kitchen Bouquet	8 to 10 medium sweet potaters
Persimmon jam	

Now, Christmas possum is different from all other possum. It's got to be caught, not killed, two weeks to a month before the cookin day. That's right around late November. You can catch 'em in the hen house, or up a 'simmon tree or in a trap. It don't make no never mind, long as he's caught live, cause they got to be penned up so you can clean 'em out. Feed 'em nothin but corn bread and milk. That'll fix 'em up, fatten 'em out, and get rid of all them no-good flavors. This makes possum as good as corn-fed pig. Then, when the time comes, kill 'em quick, skin the rascal an git shed of all the insides.

Now you got a possum ready for cookin. Sink 'em in a 'namel dish pan or basin and make sure he's good an covered. Then add a half cup of vinegar and let it soak in the icebox overnight. In the morning drain off the water and cut up the possum into rabbit pieces. Thata way the city folk'll never know they eatin possum. An I'ma tellin ya it works. Boil the possum pieces in enough salted water until it's done, but not fallin off the bone. This timin depends on the age of the possum. Sometimes it's ready in a hour, other times it'll take two. When it's done, fish out the pieces and drain 'em. That'll git ridda just about all the possum grease. When it's cool, so you can handle it, rub the rabbit-size possum pieces with salt and black pepper. Plenty. Then make a mixture of Kitchen Bouquet and half a jar of persimmon jam. I always make my jam just after the first frost cause then it's sweeter, that is, if the possums ain't done et 'em all. Just a teaspoon or two of the Kitchen Bouquet and stir it into the jam. Now, if you ain't got persimmon jam, any light tastin one'll do. Smear the stuff all over the pieces until you've got 'em coated good. Lay on four or five slices of salt pork or bacon and surround it with ya greased sweet potaters. Put it in a hot oven at 350 degrees and roast, covered, for thirty minutes. Then uncover it and cook till it's sizzlin browned but never burned (about another thirty minutes). Spoon the juice up on it every few minutes while it's uncovered. I don't think I know a soul that don't surround their possum with sweet potaters, cause it takes just about a good hour for 'em to bake. Be extry shore ya possum is done. They ain't nothing in the world worst than bein accused of servin half-baked possum.

SHOULDER ROAST OF PORK

1 pork shoulder	½ cup brown sugar
Garlic	¼ cup of bourbon
Flour, enough to dust	whiskey
it good	4 or 5 dashes of
2 Tbs of Crisco	Worcestershire sauce
½ cup French's mustard	Salt and pepper

Take your fresh shoulder and rub it round with a little bit of mashed garlic (not too much cause it'll hide the taste of the pork). Do same with salt and pepper. Wrap it up and let it sit in the icebox at least two hours (all night's best). After that dust it all up with flour and fry it rich and brown on all sides in Crisco. Dutch oven's best for this. Put the mustard in a bowl with brown sugar and add the Worcestershire sauce and whiskey, stirrin. Mix and smear on the roast and put a lid on it. Tight. If you ain't got a tight pot, seal it in tinfoil. Bake in the oven at 200 degrees or 225 degrees for 6 hours or so. If you put it in the stove just before you go to bed Christmas Eve it'll be ready by mornin. With this you ain't got to worry about raw pork, plus it's juicy. All the work's done overnight. It's like havin a Sanny Claws helper.

MADAME BUDDER WHO'S OPRY FUDGE

2 cups sugar
1 cup evaporated milk
½ tsp salt
1 Tbs margarine
1 tsp vanilla

½ cup marshmallow
  creme
½ cup chopped candied
  cherries

Combine in a heavy saucepan the sugar, milk, and salt. Heat over medium heat, stirring constantly till sugar dissolves and mixture comes to a boil. Cook to soft ball stage, and stir only if you have to. Take off the fire, add margarine and cool to warm. Don't stir. Add vanilla and beat till it begins to hold its form. Mix in the marshmallow creme, beat till very thick and starts to get dull. Fold in the cherries very fast and spread it out in a big greased platter. Mark it off in squares while it's still soft and warm. Then cut when it hardens.

COOKED APPLES

5 large cookin apples
1 cup sugar
1 tsp cinnamon

¼ tsp nutmeg
¼ cup butter
2 Tbs water

Combine sugar, cinnamon, and nutmeg. Peel apples and cut into chunks. Sprinkle sugar over apples and mix thoroughly. Put seasoned apples, butter, and water into pot, cover, and cook over low heat, stirring once or twice, for 20 minutes or until apples are tender.

These can be as good as sweet potatoes when you serve 'em with the pork.

SWEET TATER PIE

1 cup mashed cooked
   sweet taters
⅔ cup sugar
2 eggs, beaten
1 cup evaporated milk

½ tsp lemon extract
½ tsp cinnamon
½ tsp salt
   An unbaked pie crust

Scald the milk and mix everything together. Pour into the unbaked pie shell and bake at 425 degrees for 20 minutes, reduce to 350 degrees and continue another 20 or so minutes. Make sure the crust is good and brown. Cool before serving. It's best warm.

JUANITA'S PINEYWOODS HOT TAMALE

1 lb hamburger
1 onion, chopped
1 can hominy, drained
1 can HOT tamales,
   chopped (make sure
   you dehusk 'em if
   they got 'em)

1 regular can ripe pitted
   olives, chopped
1 can cream of chicken
   soup
½ pint sour cream
   Salt and pepper

Brown the hamburger and onion with salt and pepper to taste. Add the hominy, tamales, olives, chicken soup and sour cream. Mix well and pour into a two-quart baking dish. Bake at 350 degrees for 30 minutes.

   Juanita learned this in school during Around the World Week. Serves 6.

SOUTHERN SNOW BALL CAKE

1 large angel food cake	1 cup sugar
2 envelopes Knox gelatin	1 cup chopped pecans
¼ tsp salt	1 large can coconut
4 envelopes Dream Whip	1 can crushed pineapple, 1 lb 4 oz size

Cut cake in half, one half for bottom layer and the other half for top layer. Dissolve two envelopes of gelatin in two teaspoons of cold water. Add one cup boiling water, stir and let stand 10 minutes. Add pineapple, salt, sugar, and nuts, and put in icebox for one hour or until firm. Mix two envelopes of Dream Whip as directed on package. Fold into gelatin mixture. Break cake into small pieces and put in a 9 x 14-inch pan. Spread half the gelatin mixture over cake then do the same with the other half cake and mixture. Then mix the other two envelopes of Dream Whip and fold in half cup coconut and spread over the top and sprinkle with the rest of the coconut. Chill for a few hours.

AUNT DECKARD'S MINCEMEAT PIE

(With Real Meat)

6 cooking apples	¾ cup grape wine (Mogan David is good)
1 lb cooked roast beef	
1 cup dark raisins, packed down	1 tsp cinnamon
1½ cups sugar	1 tsp cloves

Stem, core (don't bother to peel) apples and slice thin. Then cut the apple slices into 8 to 10 pieces. Cut the cooked roast into small pieces about the same size as the apple pieces. Mix all ingredients (except spices—add them last) and let stand overnight or for a week in the refrigerator. Put in a pie crust, cover with top crust and bake 350 degrees for 45 minutes to a hour.

COUSIN PAT'S BIG SCRUB AMBROSIA

Add together in a bowl fresh oranges, grapefruit, coconut, and some canned pineapple—it helps cut the grapefruit if it happens to be on the tart side. Always serve in those green dishes, the ones you got for premiums at the gas station.

HOLIDAY ICEBOX CAKE

2 cups fresh cranberries, chopped
1 large banana, sliced
⅔ cup sugar
2 cups crushed vanilla wafers

½ cup butter
1 cup confectioners sugar
2 eggs
½ cup chopped pecans
1 9-oz size Cool Whip

Mix together cranberries, banana, and two thirds cup of sugar. Set aside. Place one half of the crushed vanilla wafers in bottom of buttered 8 x 8-inch glass pan. Cream butter and confectioners sugar together, add eggs and beat well. Spread this mixture over the crumbs. Now top with the cranberry mixture and sprinkle with the chopped nuts. Spread the Cool Whip over the cranberries and chopped nuts. Cover with the remaining crushed wafers, and chill at least 4 hours or overnight.

CRIMSON TIDE CHERRY SALAD

1 can sour pie cherries, drain and reserve juice
1 Tbs lemon juice
Soda water
1 cup sugar
1 small envelope unflavored gelatin
2 Tbs cold water

1 6-oz package cherry Jello
1¾ cup soda water
1 cup sliced celery
1 cup sliced stuffed olives
1 small package cream cheese, make 13 balls

With cherry juice, add lemon juice and enough soda for two cups. Mix sugar and bring to a boil. Dissolve gelatin in cold water and stir into the heated mixture. Just add the cherry Jello straight to the hot liquid. Stir until dissolved. Mix one and three quarters cups soda water and chill until starts to get thick. Lightly stir in cherries, celery and olives. Pour into a greased mold. Poke down the balls of cheese here and there. Chill until firm and unmold.

Makes one 7-cup mold.

AUNT WANNY'S CHRISTMAS RICE CREAM

1½ cups cooked rice
2 cups evaporated milk
6 egg yolks, beaten
1 cup sugar
Pinch of salt
2 tsp almond extract

6 egg whites, beaten stiff
2 cans whole cranberry sauce
2 Tbs orange juice
½ cup light brown sugar

Heat milk and sugar. Stir in egg yolks and cook till starts to thicken. Add rice, salt and continue to cook. Stir constantly until again thick. Then set off the fire and cool to warm. Add extract and fold in the stiffly beaten egg whites. Pour into a buttered baking dish and bake at 350 degrees for 20 or so minutes or until firm and slightly browned on the top. Cool or chill and top with Sanny Claws Sauce.

Sanny Claws Sauce: heat cranberries, orange juice and sugar till all is dissolved. Pour over the Christmas Rice Cream when ready to serve. Serves 10.

SANNY CLAWS SALAD

3 envelopes Knox gelatin
1 cup sugar
1 cup light brown sugar
½ cup water
  Pinch or two of salt
1 cup celery, sliced thin
1 small grapefruit,
  peeled and sectioned

1 orange, peeled and
  sectioned
1 quart bag fresh
  cranberries, cleaned
1 cup pecans, chopped
1 8-oz can crushed
  pineapple

Grind together the cranberries, grapefruit and the orange. Add to the water and sugar and cook until dissolved. Add the gelatin and mix until dissolved. Add all else and mix. Pour into a Jello mold or flat pan and chill. Serve on lettuce leaves with a spoon of mayonnaise and a cherry on top.

PLAIN OLD GUINEA DRESSING

4 cups day-old corn
  bread, crumbled
1 sleeve coarse crumbled
  saltines
½ stick oleo
1 yellow onion, chopped

½ cup celery, chopped
1 tsp ground sage
½ tsp salt
½ tsp black pepper
½ tsp poultry seasoning
  Chicken juice

Mix crackers and corn bread together with everything except the juice and mix well. Pour juice, a little at a time, until moist but not soupy. Bake at 350 degrees until brown but not dry.

This is enough dressing to go with 2 or 3 baked guineas. Double it if you want more.

AUNT NAOMI'S BAKED HAM

1 15-lb ham, precooked
Whole cloves
¼ cup pineapple/orange
juice
1 Tbs cornstarch
¾ cup brown sugar

1 Tbs French's mustard
1 small can sliced
pineapple
1 small jar Maraschino
cherries

Cook ham in water. Drain. Take off all the fat except a thin layer. Sit ham, fat side up, in a shallow baking dish. Cut diamond shapes across the back of the ham and stick each with a piece of clove. Mix juice, cornstarch, sugar, and mustard. Spread over ham. Place pineapple rings on ham and put a cherry in the middle of each hole. Bake in a 250-degree oven until the glaze bubbles, about 30–40 minutes.

This's also a MUST at Easter with potato salad and asparagus.

GREEN BEANS AND NEW POTATOES

3 lbs of fresh snapped
and stringed green
beans, any variety

2 lbs of new potatoes,
little tiny ones
3 ham hocks

In a big pot of water (the amount you think would cover the beans) boil down the ham hocks until they are tender. Add the potatoes and beans and cook till tender. If you like your beans a little crispy add them when the potatoes are almost done. Drain bean liquor and save for corn bread eatin.

CHEYENNE PACETTI'S HOLIDAY FRUIT SALAD

Pineapple, chunks or
crushed, in its own
juice (put in first so
apples don't turn
brown)

Apples, cut in bite-size
chunks
Pecans, pieces or halves
Cherries
Coconuts, shredded

Put it all in a bowl. Use your own amounts.

OLD MRS HOLLEY'S WHITE FRUITCAKE

4 cups shelled pecans
¾ lb candied cherries
1 lb candied pineapple
1¾ cups all-purpose flour
½ lb oleo

1 cup granulated sugar
5 large eggs
½ tsp baking powder
½ oz lemon extract
½ oz vanilla extract

Chop nuts and fruits into medium-size pieces. Dredge with a small amount of the flour, about a quarter cup. Cream oleo and sugar until light and fluffy. Add well beaten eggs and blend well. Sift remaining flour and baking powder together. Fold into eggs and oleo mixture. Add vanilla and lemon extracts. Mix well. Add fruits and nuts. Blend well. Grease a 10-inch tube pan or 2 loaf pans. Line with heavy brown paper and grease again. Pour batter into prepared pan or pans. Place in a cold oven and bake at 250 degrees for 3 hours for tube pan or 2 hours for 2 loaf pans. Cool in pan or pans on cake rack.

Makes 5 pounds.

HAWG KILLINS

HAWG KILLIN ACCORDIN TO UNCA T.C.

Don't let nobody tell ya it's easy. But, when you get ready, you got to kill 'em quick. But, first, let me tell you about a little fishin trip. (Aunt Evie got up and left the front porch in disgust.) I loaded up my boat and old kicker in the back of my truck and took off for Pineywoods Island fish camp. You know, Aunt Erma Lee's boy, Sebert, runs it. I got there early and bought me some bait and he help me put my boat in the water. The tide was real low. I putted on out to Cabbage Creek and fished for two or three hours. Not a bite. So, I reeled in and started to head back to the camp. When I got back to where Little Pineywoods Creek empties into Big Cabbage Creek, what do you think I see? An ol sow with two young shoats swimmin right down the creek. I hadn't caught a fish er nothin, so I thought I might catch me a little pork. I hate to go home empty-handed. I wheeled the boat around and tried to head 'em off in the water. Cause I knew if they got to land, they was long gone. The sow and one shoat broke away an hit the bank, pourin the coal to it. But the other shoat went right out, smack dab, in the middle of the big creek and started a swimmin like he was headin for New York. I knew he couldn't make it, so I decided to go after him. When I did catch up with 'em, I reached down and grabbed an ear and a leg an threw 'em in my boat. Well, he almost beat the bottom out of it and just about made me jump overboard before I could get my hands on 'em and, what else but, hawg tie 'em. I made it back to the fish camp with him a flam-a-de-bamin the boat and pulled up to the dock where Sebert was standin. I looked up at 'em and said, "What the hell kinda bait did you sell me, Sebert? Look what I done caught." He look right back at me and, without as much as takin a breath, said, "You ol fool, you, it weren't the bait it's that number-three hook and slidin sinker. It'll catch 'em every time."

After four weeks of corn, acorns and a good hard frost, I butchered my catch of the day. An Mumma made a Pig Pickin Cake, 'specially for the occasion.

PIG PICKIN CAKE

1 box Duncan Hines
  yellow cake mix
1 can of Mandarin
  oranges, drained

1 package Jello Instant
  Vanilla Pudding
1 tub Cool Whip
1 can of crushed
  pineapple, drained

Mix up your cake like it says on the box. Stir in the drained orange pieces, put in a cake pan and bake. Dump pudding in Cool Whip and mix good. Fold in drained pineapple and refrigerate to cool before icing the cake.

But the first thing I do after the hawg's butchered is take the tail pieces down to Verna May to make us a Pigtail Perlow.

VERNA MAY'S PIGTAIL PERLOW

4 or 5 pigs' tails (you might
  want to chop 'em up
  but the kids like 'em
  whole)
1 large onion, chopped

Salt to taste
Black pepper to taste
1 pinch of sugar
1 to 2 cups of uncooked rice

Fry down your salted and peppered tails until they are good and brown. Add onions and do the same. When onions are brown, add enough water to cover. Simmer slow until the tails are tender. Add rice and bring to rolling boil. If the water doesn't cover the rice by a quarter inch, add more. Put a lid on your pot and turn the fire down to slow. Cook 15 minutes, check seasonin, and stir. If it's too dry, add a little more water. If it's too wet, put a tiny crack in the lid and it'll dry out some. This is one the kids love, cause they can have so much fun gettin the meat off the tail.

After I git that a-goin, I take to the other end and start on the head. And this is my favorite thing of the hawg killin. The Hawg's Head Cheese. They's as many different ways to make it as they is hawgs' heads, but I like it plain and simple like this:

HAWG'S HEAD CHEESE

1 hog's head
1 hog's tongue
Sage
Pinch of allspice
2 or 3 whole cloves

Chili pepper or red
pepper
Vinegar
Salt and black pepper

Scrape and clean your hog's head, and trim and wash your tongue.
In a big pot, cover with salty water, allspice and cloves and simmer
until that meat leaves the bone. Drain and pick the head clean.
Shred or grind all the meat including the tongue. I like to throw
in a little bit of the ear gristle in mine. Season with the sage as
strong as you like it and as hot as you want with the red pepper.
Add a spoon or two of vinegar, salt and black pepper, and pack it
in a bowl. Cover it and put a weight on it to mash out some of the
fat and compress the meat. Some folks tie it up in cheesecloth and
squeeze it. Either way works. Put it right in the icebox and let it
stand for three days before you eat it. Then it'll slice up nice.

Now, that's it for the head and the tail. So, we'll go for the feet
next. That's one of the tastiest parts on the hog. And they so easy.
Most people just throw'em to the dawgs and don't bother with 'em,
but not me. I fix 'em two different ways, dependin on my cravin.
My first choice is pickled, cause I like 'em with a canna beer. But
they also good, what they called, deviled. I think Miss Anna
showed me how to fix 'em thata way years ago and she's kinda a
fancy woman.

PICKLED PIG'S FEET

1 tsp whole cloves
4 bay leaves
4 cups white vinegar
1 Tbs salt
1 tsp sugar

1 large onion, sliced
1 hot green pepper,
 whole
Black pepper to taste

Take all four feet. Clean and scrap 'em till they spotless. Put in a pot and cover 'em with salted water and boil 'em until the meat is ready to come away from the bone. But don't let it. Don't forget to flip off the hoofs. In a pot go ahead and mix the vinegar, cloves, bay leaves, salt, sugar, onion, hot green pepper and black pepper. Cook to a boil for 20 or 30 minutes. Add 2 cups of the foot juice to the vinegar and stir. Put your feet in a jar so as they stand, if you can, and pour the vinegar over them. Cover and let 'em sit in the icebox for 3 days to a week. The longer the better.

MISS ANNA'S DEVILED PIG'S FEET

6 pig feet
½ cup celery, chopped
2 medium onions, sliced
1 carrot, diced

1 tsp thyme
3 bay leaves
¼ tsp red pepper
⅓ tsp of black pepper

I always ended up with 4 or 8 feet. I don't know how her recipe called for 6. I guess they threw 2 to the dogs. Anyway, put everything in a pot and cover with water. Simmer till tender, about 3 hours and a few minutes. Let the feet cool off in the pot. Then take out the loose bones from them and split long ways. Dowse in cornmeal and fry, or oven-broil till they are crispy and golden. I smear 'em with mustard and eat 'em. I think Anna just threw out that juice, but I season it up or down, whichever it needs, and I got me a soup.

We took care of the outside of the hawg, now we got to go inside. And the first thing that comes to my mind is the chittlins.

It's part of the intestines. So, you got to salt 'em and wash 'em and drain 'em, till they ain't no more water in the well. Then they clean enough to eat.

MAMA ELLEN'S FRIED CHITTLINS

Cut cleaned chittlins into small pieces and boil in salted water until tender. Drain off all the water. Salt, pepper and roll in cracker meal or cornmeal. Fry till golden and crispy.

Then you got what the old timers called hog lights. It ain't really no kinda light, it's the liver and the lungs. An it makes the best kinda stew. And with the liver you can make liver mush if you just want to make the stew outta the lungs.

HOG LIGHTS STEW

1 set of hog lights	Salt and black pepper
1 large onion, chopped	to taste
2 toes garlic, chopped	Flour

Chop your lights up into bite-size pieces. Fry down in heavy pot with the onion and the garlic till it is brown. Add water to cover, salt and pepper, and stew till tender. If it's not thick enough for you, use a little flour to make it thicker. Spoon that over rice and some Scratch Backs on the side, and you're fixed.

MUMMA PAT'S SCRATCH BACKS

This takes coarse ground cornmeal and a handful of cracklins. To the cornmeal and cracklins, add salt and enough boiling water to make it thick as putty. By hand, make small half inch thick pones. Fry till crispy and brown. Eat 'em hot slicked down with butter, if you got it. They so good and crunchy, they scratch your backbone goin down.

UNCA T.C.'S LIVER MUSH

1 hog liver, cut up,
    washed and picked
    clean of the
    membranes
¾ cups coarse ground
    cornmeal

Salt
Black pepper
1 Tbs thyme
1 Tbs sage
1 tsp flake red pepper

Cook liver in salted water until tender. Drain and mash to a paste. Make a sluice of the liver and one cup of the liver juice. Put in pot and bring up to a boil while adding the cornmeal, till it gits good and thick. Add seasonings. Scrape into a mold of some kind and let it get cold. Remove and slice. It's a meal in one.

For the most part, everything else is just one cut of meat or another. Shoulders, hams, chops, ribs and bacon meat. Then, after that, the rest you fry down to render your lard. And that's where you git the cracklins. But, sometimes, I git a wild hair and I'll make the whole damn thing in sausage and it's done with. But I'll give it to you for a small batch.

MISS ANNA'S HOMEMADE SAUSAGE

2 lbs fresh lean pork
¼ lb fat
½ tsp thyme
1½ tsp sage
½ tsp celery seed

½ tsp allspice
1 tsp black pepper
1½ tsp salt
1 tsp vinegar

Grind up the meat and the fat together. Add the spices and mix with your hands. You can make patties or stuff it.

What I like to do with this is make me a big pan of Dirty Rice. My brother raised coon dogs in Louisiana and he told me how to do this.

UNCA CLARENCE'S DIRTY RICE

1 lb fresh loose sausage	3 toes garlic, squashed
½ lb cooked hogs liver or any kind	Cayenne to taste
	Salt
2 large onions, chopped	2 cups rice

Fry the sausage, onion and garlic till brown. Add crumbled up hogs liver. Season and put in the rice. Add water to cover and boil for one or two minutes. Turn down the fire and simmer until the rice is dry.

After all this smellin-up of the kitchen, cooking heads, feet and chittlins, you couldn'ta sleeped if Mama hadn'ta come and cooked a batch of Pickled Up Peaches and some Butter And Bread Pickles. This sweetened the house right back. And I can tell you word for word how she did it. (Aunt Evie came to the screen door, puckered her lip and left again.)

AUNT EVIE'S PICKLED PEACHES

18–20 small to medium peeled peaches	2 cups vinegar
¼ cup whole cloves	4½ cups sugar
	3 cinnamon sticks

Boil the sugar, cinnamon, vinegar, and cloves for 15 minutes. Save enough cloves to stick two or three in each peach. Then drop peaches a little bit at a time into the mixture and cook them till they are tender but not overcooked. Put peaches in hot-scalded jars and fill with the peach juice. Make sure that every jar gits a few cloves and a stick of cinnamon.

Three to four quarts depending on the size of the peaches.

AUNT EVON'S BUTTER AND BREAD PICKLES

4 quarts medium cucumbers, sliced	3 cloves garlic, chopped
	1/3 cup coarse salt
6 medium white onions, sliced	5 cups sugar
	3 cups cider vinegar
2 sweet green peppers, chopped	1½ tsp turmeric
	1½ tsp celery seed

Bring your sugar, vinegar, turmeric, and celery seed to a boil. Drop in everything else and bring back to a small boil (don't boil heavy), then jar 'em in scalded jars and seal them.

AUNT WANNY'S WATERMELON PRESERVES

1 lb watermelon rind	2 cups sugar
Water	½ lemon
2 Tbs lime (calcium oxide)	

Trim off outer green skin and pink flesh, using only greenish white parts of rind. Cut rind into one-inch cubes, and weigh. Dissolve the lime in two quarts water. Soak cubes for three and a half hours in lime water. Drain and place cubes in clear water for an hour. Again, drain off water and boil one and a half hours in fresh water, then drain. Make a syrup of two cups of sugar and one quart water. Add rind and boil one hour. As syrup thickens, add half a lemon, thinly sliced. When the syrup begins to thicken and the melon is clear, the preserves are ready. Pack them into hot sterilized jars, add enough syrup to cover, and seal.

While mama was doin this I'd git me a half a water glass of my latest homemade grape or berry wine and ease myself right on down into the evenin. You know, they weren't no such thing as TV back then.

UNCA T.C.'S HOMEMADE WINE

(Doubles Good)

3 pints grapes or berries
3 lbs sugar

Rinse and mash fruit. Mix sugar with enough water to dissolve it and add grapes or berries. Finish off a one gallon jar almost to the top with cold water. Cap it loose like and let stand for about 6 weeks. Strain, re-bottle, and stash it. It's best in a cool place in the summer.

SEWIN, QUILTIN, TACKY AND HOME DEMONSTRATION PARTIES

COVINA'S CLUTCH

Everyone showed up on Mrs. Covina Wright's front porch at the same time. The ladies, ever so slightly, elbowed each other, gently nudging, to get to her door. They were all anxious and twitching to show off their favorite prepared dishes that teetered in one hand, while a treasured bag of quilting scraps was clutched tight in the other. And there wasn't one of them that didn't have a giant pocketbook hooked in the crook of her arm. With everybody carrying handbags, scrap bags and casseroles, it was right crowded on the porch and a fidgety mess. After all, it was a day that the members of the Two Egg Quilting and Public Speaking Club waited for each week. Since, they all looked up to Covina, impressing her was of the utmost importance. She was the widow of the local undertaker and had been a comforting hostess at the funeral parlor until her husband died. Before that, she was a very well thought of schoolteacher. However, above all else that fascinated them with Covina was, they knew she had a little money. So, when the quilting was held at her house the girls always tried to do their very best.

Mrs. Wright was waiting for the group in her parlor. She heard the noise on the porch and hurried to open the front door before any of them could take a vote on "who would knock". It was too late. They had all knocked at the same time. When she opened the door the ladies had already lodged themselves in it. Covina's mind pictured a flock of guinea hens, all trying to get through the same hole in a fence. Then, her face went blank as she gazed out into the 'maylange' of hats and frocks from the Diana Shop swooshing against each other. Pocketbooks and shoes from Becks tapped and clicked together with a clink-a-dee-clank, that came, from what must have been a foot tub of Sarah Coventry jewelry. Mrs. Wright felt sure someone had dumped it on them as they came up the sidewalk and it stuck at random. But on top of all this was the cloud of Avon. Every scent ever produced. Covina's nose, particularly, twicked on the ancient smell of Tabu, "so old it had gone off," she thought. Then, out of the stacks of casserole dishes, pie plates, cake pans and mounds of tinfoil-covered things, came the scrumptious smell of food. It dominated everything and reminded Covina of the main reason for having a quilting party. Eating. The ladies always, nonchalantly, rushed through the business to get to the eating part of the meeting, even Covina.

May Ben Robbins broke the door jam first. She busted loose and headed straight for the kitchen, squealing, while in route, "mine's got to be put on the bottom rack of the oven, cause the top rack's too hot." "Mine goes up nex ta the broiler. It's got ta be browned real good," piped another. "Move out of my way, I got to get to the icebox, if you don't mind," sassily demanded another. And it went on and on until Beulah Harris, a foot taller than anybody there, and wearing what appeared to the ladies as men's clothes, spoke up and said, "I don't care where you put mine, but you better take it NOW, 'fore I put it some place you ain't gone want it." Beulah made a loud laugh and that ended it. She loved agitating the prissier ones. At once, they scattered and regrouped again in the quilting room and without hesitation started pulling on their wads of scraps. Every member of the club had her own handmade bag, personally sewn from some sort of tapestry or other fine material, which she used to carry her precious remnants. And, weekly, each tried to out-do the other by bringing the most beautiful or outlandish piece of fabric that could be found. While the others were digging, Beulah eased her large swath of black-and-white velvet print out of her paper sack. Covina spied the piece from across the room. She went directly to Beulah and, with her fingers rubbing the textured flocked velvet, she said, "This is it. The very piece we need to go on and finish our patterin." The other ladies didn't have a chance to look up, before Covina announced it was all over, like a queen making a decree. The group clucked with contempt, but knew Mrs. Covina Wright, with all that money, had taste and must be right. So, they went along with it. In five minutes the chosen piece was cut into about seventeen smaller ones (they loved hacking it up) and the sewing had begun. Covina was quick to remind them that the quilt must be finished today, since it was to be a wedding present, this coming week, for the daughter of the local preacher. The girls sewed with a little resentment in each stitch, mainly because Beulah's material was chosen. They were also hungry and no one really liked the preacher's daughter to begin with. It was Covina's 'idear' to give the quilt to the new bride but they still didn't like her. Anyway, they were sewing so hard no one paid a bit of attention to the design on the outrageous fabric. Beulah worked as quickly as the others knowing that, shortly, the quilt would be finished, folded, put in a box and wrapped. Soon, she would be as tickled as any to have that old scrap of hers dominating the top of the preacher's daughter's quilt.

It wasn't long before Covina cleared her throat and in her refined girls' school voice, as mistress of ceremony, said that it was time for the two speakers of the week to share their talk about a recent experience with the rest of the club. She quickly reminded Willadoll Roundtree Peaster and Beulah Harris that the speech was to be short, to the point, and directed at the members. They drew needles. Beulah got the longest one, so Willadoll was picked to go first. Reluctantly, she stood up by her place at the quilting frame and made a kind of goat sound, then hesitated. Mrs. Wright immediately said, while thinking about the food in the kitchen, "Come on, Willadoll, cat got your tongue?"

In a voice a little above a whisper and looking straight down she said, "I's down to Williston the other day at a restrent where my sister waits on tables." Covina interrupts, "Miseres Peaster, don't talk to the quilt now." Willie didn't like it but looked up and went on, "She tol me that Lacy Blodgett was rushed ta the Williston Hospital in so bad a shape they couldn't mov'er else she'd a died. My sister said, them doctors down there cut her open an took out er heart. Put it on a plane an flew it to Arlanduh in a beer cooler. They fixed that thing an flew it back while Lacy laid up there half dead, waitin for her heart to come back from Disney World. She said, they put it in an sewed er up 'fore the plane'od lef the groun. She's walkin all over Williston now jes like nuthin ever hap'emed. It ain't no tellin what them doctors is a libel to do nex." As Willadoll sat down, each lady turned to the next and mumbled something so low nobody else could hear it. But for Covina, there was no one to tell what she wanted. So she said, not knowing what else to say, "My, that was a very intristing story, Willadoll. Thank you very much."

Beulah was already nervous because she knew that Mrs. Wright didn't waste any time between talks and she was next. "Well, Beulah, it's your turn," she said, while thinking what kind of incredible story will I hear from this one. Beulah didn't wait a second, she stood up, gazed out the window and began, "Las week I took it on myself to find me a restin place. A cemetery plot. Y'all knowed I los my husban in a fishin accident and they never found 'is body so, I ownly need a place for me to be buried. I checked the newspaper and the television ads to see who had a nice cheap lot. But they was, all, too fancy or too expensive. On that, I called Wee Jean Watters," as she looks at her sitting down on the other end of the quilting frame. "I thought she might know of a place for me in my price range. I knew that her husban had sold cemetery plots, at one time, while he was in between jobs. So, she was the one to call. Well, Wee Jean said she knew just the place to look, but it was way up on the north end of the county. Now, knowing Wee Jean like I do, I knowed she'd tell ya just about anything ta git to go for a ride. But, I picked'er up anyways and we headed out. We was nearly to Jawga when we came upon this little hill that had a scatterin of scrub oaks on it. And I could tell by the look on her face that this was the spot. It had a hogwire fence and cattlegap gate, with a big wooden sign that said, COUNTRYLAWN CEMETERY. It was nuthin. An ol cow pasture. But Wee Jean kep at me till I got out of the car and walked round. I had to to shut'er up. She didn't say two words the whole time, but when we got back to the car she asked me if I liked it. So, I just lit in. Wee Jean, I said, I'd ruther be drug out on a hill and let the buzzards eat me than to be buried there. I've been shit on all my life and I ain't about to pay and be shit on by no bunch of cows forever after." Beulah sat down, laughing.

At first, no one could figure out whether she was finished or just quit in the middle, but Covina quickly seized the moment, in order to save the ladies from embarrassment. She offhandedly thanked Beulah and hurried on with the meeting. "The quilt is finished and ready to wrap. Please, don't anyone forget to sign the card. We want everyone to know who did all the hard work," she said. Each signed it and, one by one, scrambled for the kitchen to get their casseroles out of the oven. It was chaos, for a few minutes, with a hot dish in every hand and no place to put them. Then,

Covina came in and arranged the vegetables together, the meats with the meats, and all the sweet things in a row. They were simply amazed at how she could organize and how everything fell into place, for her. With that, they all gathered together, now feeling a closeness as they stood in line, ready to heap their plates. Even Covina.

When the time came round that next week for a meetin, everything had changed. The quilting club had broken up—and Mrs. Wright had disappeared.

You see, Covina generously offered to take the present to the shower for the ladies. And she did, right up to the front of the room. The preacher's daughter quickly tore off the pretty paper and ripped opened the box. The quilt was neatly folded and had the card on top. She picked it up and read all the names of the ladies aloud and thanked Mrs. Wright for all of them, since they weren't there. She grabbed the quilt and shook it out on a large, wide table where the shower-goers could see it. A quilt from the club was a prestigious gift in these parts. The ladies were famous for their handwork and their food. So, they were all filing by, to get a gander at it, when three of the staunchest and hardest shelled members of the Mount Olive Baptist Church went weak-kneed and started screaming. They dabbed and comforted themselves with kleenexes, little balled-up pieces of paper and handkerchiefs, while exclaiming what had dissolved them to this state. One hollered, "My Gawd, only the Devil himself would do it! It's filthy!" Another shrieked, "The hands of those women are the hands of Beasabub! I knew it all the time!" And the one dabbing the most with the kleenex said, "It looks ta me like a can of necked worms . . . doin it! Oh . . . my . . . Gawd!" The preacher's daughter didn't move. She stood there with a blank look on her face and still couldn't see what they were all carrying on about. Cautiously, Covina peeped over their shoulders to see exactly what had set off the hysteria. There, right on top of the quilt, was that black-and-white piece of flocked velvet, clearly, depicting a Roman Orgy. How she could have missed seeing it she didn't know, but there was no mistake. It was in bold print. Without considering anything, which was next to impossible for Covina, she made a dash for her coat and gloves, and was gone before anyone could miss her. At home, she threw some things into her suitcase and left, on a sudden vacation, with one thing on her mind. Beulah Harris.

And, to this day, Beulah swears that she didn't know a "thiiiing about it."

MAY BEN ROBBIN'S ORIENTAL OVEN PERLOW

1½ cups uncooked rice
2 Tbs margarine
½ cup onions, sliced thin
¾ cup celery, sliced thin
1 large green pepper, cut in long strips
1 can bamboo sprouts, drained
1 can water chestnuts, drained

3 chicken bouillon cubes, any kind
3 cups of water
3 Tbs soy sauce
1½ tsp salt
½ tsp pepper
1¼ cups almonds, slivered

Melt margarine in a pot and cook onions until limp. Add everything else but the rice and nuts and cook till hot but don't let it boil. Put the rice in a dry black iron skillet and toast it on top of the stove, stirring often. Put browned rice in a baking dish big enough to hold everything and pour the liquid on the rice and add the almonds to the top. Put on a tight lid and bake at 350 degrees for 50 minutes or until the liquid is all gone. If too dry add a little more water.

May Ben promises you: they'll think you've been to China.
Serves 6.

MISS DICYS RICHMAN'S RICE

1¾ cups cooked rice	2 Tbs chopped onion
1 cup grated cheese	3 eggs
¾ cup chopped parshly	Salt and pepper

Mix the rice, cheese, parshly, onion, egg yolks (savin aside the whites) and salt and pepper. Beat whites till stiff and stir into the rice. Turn into a greased one-quart baking dish and cook at 350 degrees for 25 minutes. Serve it while it's hot.

Serves 4.

QUICK LORETTA

1 unbaked pie shell	2 cups evaporated milk
10 slices of bacon, fried crisp	½ onion, chopped
1 cup grated white cheese	½ green bell pepper, chopped
4 eggs	Small jar of pimientos

Crumble the bacon in the bottom of the pie crust. Sprinkle with grated cheese. Mix the other ingredients together and pour over the pie. Bake for 35 minutes at 375 degrees.

Makes 6 nice slices.

BEULAH HARRIS'S DOUBLE FREEZED ICE CREAM

2 cups evaporated milk
1 tsp unflavored Knox
   gelatin
¼ cup Karo syrup

1 tsp vanilla extract
⅓ cup sugar
2 pinches of salt

Take a half cup of the milk and sprinkle the Knox over it and let it sit for 5 minutes. Then place over low fire and stir until the gelatin has completely dissolved. Move off the heat and stir in the vanilla, salt, syrup and sugar. Then blend the remaining one and a half cups milk into the mixture. Pour into ice tray and freeze hard (approximately one hour). Remove from freezer and make small chunks of the ice cream in a chilled bowl. Beat with a electric mixer until creamy, but not melted. Pour it back in the ice tray and freeze hard, two hours at the least.

WILLADOLL'S BAKED PEEKABEEF

1 lb ground meat
2 Tbs cooking oil
3 stalks celery, chopped
2 medium onions,
   chopped
1 can cream of chicken
   soup
1 can golden mushroom
   soup

1 soup can of evaporated
   milk
1 small package of egg
   noodles
1 can chow mein noodles
½ cup toasted and salted
   pecan bits

In the oil, brown the onions, celery and meat. Stir soups and milk into the meat and mix well. Prepare noodles according to the package and mix into the beef. Pour into a big baking dish and cook, covered, at 350 degrees for about one hour. Uncover and sprinkle on the chow mein noodles and pecan bits, return to the oven for 10 more minutes.

WEE JEAN'S TURNIPED SAUSAGE CASSEROLE

½ lb loose pork sausage
1 medium head celery,
  chopped
/ green onions, chopped
  with tops
1 large sweet green
  pepper, chopped

2 packages dry chicken
  noodle soup
1 cup rice
4½ cups water, boiling
1 cup diced turnips
½ cup pecans

Lightly brown sausage. Pour off all but 3 tablespoons of the grease. Cook onions, celery, and green pepper in the sausage till tender. Salt and pepper to taste. Add the rice and soup to the boiling water and cook seven minutes. Drop in the turnips. Then mix everything together and pour into big baking dish. Cover with the pecans, put on a tight lid and cook in a 350-degree oven for one hour and fifteen minutes. Take off the lid for the last 15 or 20 minutes.

"It'll feed 'em all. But you better have all your quiltin done," Wee Jean emphasized.

EULLA PULLEN'S FIG NEWTON CREME

(Dana's Sister)

15 Fig Newtons
1 large can fruit cocktail,
  drained
1 Tbs lemon juice

1 tsp vanilla
1½ cups heavy whipping
  cream (put in freezer
  for 20 minutes)

Pinch each Fig Newton into fours. Mix with fruit cocktail, lemon juice, and vanilla. Whip the cream till stiff, fold into the fig mixture and serve chilled.

Serves 6.

LAYCINE DEATS'S DEEP DISH DEVIL CRAB

1 yellow onion, diced
1 medium sweet pepper, diced
2 eggs
1 stick oleo
1 lb crab meat, drained and flaked
1 cup corn bread crumbs
1 tsp French's mustard
2 tsp Worcestershire sauce
1 can golden mushroom soup
1 Tbs dry sherry wine
3 Tbs lemon juice, fresh

Fry down the pepper and onions in half of the oleo till soft. Mix all other ingredients except the eggs and corn bread crumbs into the onions and pepper. Beat up the eggs and add to this also. At once slip it all down in a good and greased deep baking dish and cover with the crumbs. Dot with what's left of the oleo and bake at 375 degrees for about 35 minutes. Make sure the crumbs, on the top, are good and brown.

Serves six ladies.

SOPHIE MAE'S PEANANA DELITE

3 smallish bananas
1 cup Sophie Mae peanut brittle, crushed
2 tsp vanilla
1½ cups whipping cream

Peel the ripe bananas and slice very thin. Fold into the whipped cream, the bananas, the peanut brittle, and the vanilla. Put in fancy glasses and chill.

Serves 4.

LORNA'S PRUNE CAKE

2 cups sugar
2 cups self-rising flour
3 eggs
1 tsp allspice
1 tsp cinnamon
1 tsp nutmeg

2 jars Gerber's Prune
   with Tapioca baby
   food
1 cup cooking oil
1 cup chopped nuts and
   raisins

Mix dry ingredients. Add remaining ingredients. Bake in funnel pan at 350 degrees until done. If you don't like the spices you can leave them out.

KATHERINE BELLE'S TOMATO SOUP CAKE

1 can tomato soup
1 cup sugar
2 Tbs oleo
1 cup raisins
1 cup candied cherries,
   chopped
1 cup nuts, chopped

1½ cups flour
1 egg
1 tsp cloves
1 tsp cinnamon
1 tsp nutmeg
1 tsp soda

Mix sugar, oleo, tomato soup and egg. Beat well. Sift flour, spices and soda. Add to the first mixture and mix. Add nuts and cherries and raisins and mix. Bake one hour in oven at 350 degrees. Use tube pan or leaf pan.

WILLADOLL'S HULA BREAD

2 cups flour
1 tsp soda
½ tsp salt
½ cup butter or
   margarine
1 cup sugar
2 eggs

1 cup mashed bananas
1 Tbs grated orange rind
¼ cup milk
1 tsp vanilla
1 cup flaked coconut
½ cup chopped pecans

Sift flour, soda, and salt. Cream the butter and sugar. Add eggs and beat it. Add mashed bananas, orange rind, milk, and vanilla. Stir it. Add dry ingredients. Mix it. Add coconut, pecans and bake it at 350 degrees for one hour and 10 minutes (or until it tests done) in a greased loaf pan.

Willadoll says, "If ya kinda wiggle a little while ya stirrin, it'll come out better."

BOBBIE'S LEMON/LIME JELLO CAKE SUPREME

1 box Duncan Hines
   Lemon Supreme Cake
   Mix

6 yard eggs
¾ cups Crisco oil
1 small box lime Jello

Dissolve Jello in 1 cup of water and add to the cake mix and blend. Add oil and blend, then one egg at a time and blend. Pour into a greased and floured tube pan and bake at 350 degrees for 1 hour. "That's Alabama time, down here in Flarda it take 30 minutes," Bobbie says.

Icing:
1 box powdered sugar
Lemon juice

Add the juice a little at the time till it's somewhere in between thick and runny. Then pour it on while the cake is still hot.

TAMMY FAYE'S TUMPED TUNA JUMP

5 potatoes, sliced
Mayonnaise
¼ cup stuffed green
 olives, chopped
1 can tuna fish, drained
 and flaked

½ cup chopped pimientos
Salt and pepper to taste
1 cup milk
1 cup crushed corn chips

Mayonnaise the potato slices and arrange (in a greased baking dish) in layers with the olives, tuna and pimientos, seasoning each layer with salt and pepper. Tump in the milk and cover with the corn chips. Bake at 400 degrees for 55 minutes. Make sure the potatoes are done before you take it out of the oven.

Perfect for a Tacky party.

ESTELL'S SHORTCUT BAKED CUSTARD

5 eggs, beaten lightly
1 can Eagle Brand
 condensed milk
3½ cups hot water
1 Tbs flour

½ tsp salt
2 tsp vanilla
Nutmeg
Margarine

Mix the Eagle brand, the flour and the hot water together. Now slowly add and stir the mixture into the eggs. Mix in the salt and the vanilla. Pour into greased custard cups, sprinkle with nutmeg and bake at 350 degrees sitting in a pan of shallow water for almost an hour. Take out of the oven and cool or chill in the icebox.

Makes 10 or 12 custard cups.

COVINA'S CURRY GREEN TOMATO CHOPS

4 good pork chops
1 large onion, sliced
2 green tomatoes, sliced

1 Tbs curry powder
Salt and pepper
Cooking sherry

In a skillet brown your salted and peppered pork chops. Place them in the bottom of a baking dish. Then layer the tomato and the onion until it's gone. Sprinkle on the curry powder, salt and pepper and a spoon or two of cooking sherry. Bake at 375 degrees for a little less than an hour.

When the girls smell the sherry in Covina's chops they all make "that" face, knowing she's trying to out-do them.

Serves 4.

CHICKEN ROSALEE

3 cups cooked chicken
meat, chunked
1 can chopped
mushrooms
⅓ cup chopped bell
pepper
½ stick margarine
2 Tbs flour

1 cup chicken juice or
bouillon
3 Tbs pimiento, chopped
2 dashes Worcestershire
sauce
1 tsp thyme
Salt and pepper to taste
½ pint sour cream

Simmer the pepper and mushrooms in the margarine and blend in the flour. Add the Worcestershire sauce, thyme, salt, pepper and the juice. Cook till thick. Add chicken and pimiento and cook for 7 more minutes. Blend in the sour cream while it's hot and serve over rice.

Serves 6.

COVINA'S PEACHES AND DREAMS

2 cups mashed peaches,
  fresh or canned
1⅓ cups sugar
1 Tbs fresh lemon juice

½ pint whipping cream,
  whipped
1 cup macaroons,
  crumbled

Mix the peaches, sugar, and the lemon juice. Fold in the whipped cream. Sprinkle the bottom of a pie tin with half of the crumbs. Pour in the peaches and dreams and cover with a blanket of remaining macaroons. Freeze 4 hours. Slices like a pie.

Will serve 6.

POST GRAPE NUTS LORRAINE

2 bacon slices
1 cup thinly sliced
  onions
3 eggs, slightly beaten
1¾ cups milk
¾ cup (3 oz) shredded
  Swiss cheese

1 tsp salt
  Dash of pepper
⅓ cup Post Grape Nuts
1 lightly baked 9-inch
  pie shell

Fry bacon. Drain and crumble. Reserve one tablespoon of drippings. Saute onions in bacon drippings until tender and browned. Combine eggs, milk, cheese, salt, pepper and cereal. Stir in onions and bacon. Pour into shell and bake at 450 degrees for 15 minutes and reduce temperature to 350 degrees and bake for 15 minutes.

FANCY-SCHMANCY TUNA NOODLE BAKE

Follow the recipe for MIDNIGHT CRUNCHY CRUMB TUNA CASSEROLE (it's on page 122), making some changes. Be sure to use solid white albacore tuna. Leave out the pimiento. Instead of cream of celery soup, use cream of asparagus. Instead of plain old egg noodles, use some color or other Italian noodles, green ones are easiest to find, but sometimes you can get a package of red, green and yellow ones. The final touch! Stir in about half a cup of Feta cheese, or even one of those French goat cheeses, and crumble some more on top before baking.

IRIS SALAD

1 can applesauce
1 pack lime Jello
1 tsp lemon juice

1 Tbs sugar
1 small bottle ginger ale

Heat applesauce and add lime Jello and sugar, and dissolve. Cool. Add lemon juice and ginger ale. Chill.

WILLISTEEN'S SHRIMP WIGGLE

4 Tbs butter
2 Tbs flour
1½ cup milk
1 cup shrimp
1 cup peas

Paprika
Celery salt
1 egg yolk
1 Tbs cooking sherry

Melt butter. Stir in flour and blend. Gradually add milk. Bring sauce to a boil and add shrimp. Simmer about 5 minutes. Add drained peas and season to taste with paprika and celery salt. While sauce is still simmering beat in the egg yolk and let it thicken slightly. Add sherry. Serve. The Wiggle can also be put in a casserole dish and covered with buttered bread crumbs then browned under the broiler. If mixture is too thick, dilute with some milk.

"It was so good Covina got on her horse crosswise," Willisteen said.

COVINA'S ANGELS ON HORSEBACK

1 pint oysters	12 slices bacon
½ tsp salt	⅛ tsp pepper
⅛ tsp paprika	2 Tbs parsley

Drain oysters and lay each across a half slice bacon. Sprinkle with seasonings and chopped parsley. Roll bacon around oyster and fasten with toothpick. Place on rack in shallow baking pan and bake in hot oven 450 degrees for about 10 minutes, or until bacon is crisp. Remove toothpicks and serve.

LACY'S SWEET CHOCOLATE PIE

4-oz package sweet chocolate	3-oz package cream cheese
⅓ cup milk	8-oz container of Cool Whip
2 Tbs sugar	1 baked and cooled pie crust

Heat chocolate and 2 tablespoons of milk in saucepan over low heat stirring until chocolate is melted. Beat sugar into cream cheese, add remaining milk and chocolate mixture. Heat until smooth. Cool slightly and fold in the Cool Whip. Spoon into crust and freeze until it's firm, about 4 hours. Garnish with chocolate curls.

SINKIN SPELLS, HOT FLASHES, FITS AND CRAVINS

GREENS COVER A MULTITUDE OF SINS

As told by Miss Minna Dean Winke, a maidenlady and librarian:

You know, I've never met anybody in Putnam County that hadn't heard something about Jeanette Rose Pink's awesome hot flashes. The family has made them legendary and they hand 'em down, too. You take her Aunt Jeanette Belle Pink. She had 'em terribler than her niece did. However they both found remedies and relief in many different ways, she said.

It was Belle that was notorious for undressing anyone and everyone within reach who looked the least bit too bundled-up. She'd grab 'em right at the onset of one of those flushed feelings as the heat started rising up her body. That's when she'd begin pulling at the blankets or clothes of the nearest one. She especially went for babies, Minna Dean said. She loved to free the neck area first. One time, while she was waiting in a checkout line at a local grocery store, it happened. She completely stripped a young'un still in the arms of its mother and never stopped hollerin, "My Gawd, that baby must be smothering to death, all wrapped up like that. Get them blankets off 'im 'fore I pass out right here from the heat." Another time, at a filling station, she jumped out of her car while it was still rolling, ran across the lot, and grabbed Carmilla Webber by the coat and scarf. They said, she pulled and pleaded desperately trying to convince Carmilla that she must be sweltering underneath such a pile of clothes.

But the incident which almost got 'em all sent to Chatahoochee, or jail, was at her oldest sister's funeral. There was poor ol Fannie, laying up in her coffin, ready to go. Belle had taken her seat in the front pew, when one of them things came over her. While she was under that devilmade fit of heat, she slipped up to the casket, and, before anyone could notice, started undoing Fannie's burial outfit at the neck. The family was in too much shock to do anything, if they cared at all. Finally the undertakers came and drug Belle away screaming, "Gawd lov er, Fannie must be heatin to death. Gawd lov er."

Now, I've got to hand it to Jeanette Rose Pink. She tried hard

not to impose on anyone when she had a spell. She vowed never to
act like Belle and tried to do different. She did, but some of her
remedies were not very ladylike. She'd do the darnedest things
right in mixed company. I've seen her, you can believe this if you
want, gather up a big handful of skirt and start fanning herself—
and I'm not talking about her face. Then, if that didn't cool things
off, she'd snatch up a piece of newspaper or cardboard, the nearest
thing, and begin to waffing it back and forth up under her dress.
She didn't care who was around! Late one night I went over to her
house to borry a cup of sugar, cause I live a couple of places down
the road from her. The back door was open so I just went. . . .
on. . . . in. Well, there she was sitting in a kitchen chair, as big
as you please, with her legs spread and straddling the open door of
the refrigerator. And, if that wasn't enough, she had the oscillating
fan going . . . you know where. I couldn't believe it. She was sleep-
ing like a baby, so I got my sugar and went home.

I'm not going to tell you the whole story but everybody knows
she's got a nightgown with breakaway buttons all the way down
the front. Some nights you can hear her to my house. She'll jump
out of bed, scream, and run, while ripping off her gown, then land
spread-eagle on top of a cold Formica table. She told somebody that
it was the only thing in the house that could, really, cool 'er off.
They tell me, if you have them hot flashes, you'll do anything to
get relief, and Jeanette Rose just about did. But the incident that
came close to putting them all in the grave, and made the inside
page of the Palatka Sun, I might add, happened while Rose's two
cousins were visiting here from Rolling Fork, Mississippi. Raenelle
and Betty Sue were at Jeanette's house waiting for her to return
from the store, when the phone rang and a mysterious voice said,
"Y'all better get down to the shopping mall and pick up Jeanette
Rose. . . . . she's passed out in the grocery store." And
hung up. They jumped in the car and drove the quarter of a mile
to the mall and ran into the store. Jeanette was just coming to when
they reached her. She was still on the floor of the supermarket, with
her coat pulled tightly closed. Betty Sue and Raenelle looked at
each other and at the two large bulges under her coat. Raenelle
flung it open to see what the lumps was. They were sure, when the
lumps turned out to be bundles of collard greens and mustard

greens, that she had been caught for shoplifting and fainted. "Cause that's what she went to store for," said Minna Dean.

Finally somebody came over and began to tell the girls what had gone on. It was a lady assistant manager who told her cousins the entire story of how Jeanette had come into the store acting real funny. "She kept on hangin around the frozen foods and walkin up and down in front of the freezers," the assistant manager said. "Then, after about an hour, she stopped, and, with her coat open, hovered over one of them small little freezers in the middle of the aisle, you know, the kind we put our specials in," she said. "Then up stepped Ms. so and so, that church lady, and asked Jeanette if everything was all right. She said she was just about to heat to death and was trying to keep cool. With that she slithered down the front of the of the freezer and fell into a dead faint. Her coat flew open as she fell back, leaving everything she had out in the open. I mean she didn't have nothin on except her high heels, panties and brazier," Minna Dean said the manager said.

It was then the bag boy rushed over and placed a bunch of greens over her chest and bunch of greens over her female organs, down there. Miss Winke claims it to be the gospel, by way of Paulette Huff, who said, "I seen it all." With that, Minna put her hand to her forehead, rolled her eyes, and bit down on her bottom lip.

———————

AUNT JEANETTE BELLE PINK'S OYSTER STEW

(Good for Anything)

2 cups sweet milk
2 cups coffee cream
5 Tbs butter (you got to
  have it for this one)
1 quart fresh shucked
  oysters and juice

1 tsp Worcestershire
  sauce
1 Tbs minced celery
1 tsp salt (more
  depending on the salt
  of the oysters)
Black pepper to taste

Put the butter in a saucepan and get it hot. Fry the celery until it is clear but not brown (careful butter burns easy). Add milk, Worcestershire sauce, salt, pepper and stir until hot. Pour in the oysters and simmer until they get firm but not shrivelled up. Put in bowl and cover the top with the little biddy round crackers.

It's enough for 6 with the cravin.

GOO FRANICE JAN'S

1½ lb Velveeta, cubed
  (There is no
  substitute!)
8 to 10 strips bacon, cooked
  crisp and drained

1 can tomato soup
Milk
Hot pepper sauce

In the top of double boiler, over simmering water, heat undiluted tomato soup. Add Velveeta gradually, until melted. Crumble bacon, large and small bits, into cheese and stir a lot. Add several drops pepper sauce if desired and a tablespoon or so of milk to thin, if too thick. Serve hot, out of pan, over saltines (preferred) or toast (if you want to be fancy).

It'll stick to anything.

Many servings.

MISS MACK'S JELLY JAR MILK SHAKES

Fill an almost empty jelly jar with two-thirds milk and shake. Drink right out of the jar. The kids just love 'em.

PATTINA BLAIR'S SICK SOUP

Warm milk on the stove. Add a hunk of butter and some sugar to taste. Make light bread toast, butter a bit, cut into pieces. Put toast pieces in a soup bowl and cover with the warm milk. It will cure you every time.

SOUP BEANS

(From the Big Scrub)

Take some white beans, cover with water and some baking soda. Bring to a boil. The water will turn yellow as bile. Pour off the water and repeat the process. Pour off the second water, rinse a bit. Add fresh water, some hunks of ham bone and bring to a boil, cover and let simmer till time to serve. No need to soak the beans overnight. The baking soda will take the meaness out of the beans. Soup Beans are even better if cooked the day before. Things after the second heating are always more flavorful, ain't they.

COVERED DOG PIZZA

1 package hot dogs	Oregano
½ lb sharp rat cheese	12 hamburger rolls

Split rolls. Chop up the hot dogs and cheese all together. Spread on rolls and sprinkle with oregano. Bake at 400 degrees for 10 to 15 minutes.
Makes 24.

MIDNIGHT CRUNCHY CRUMB TUNA CASSEROLE

1 small can tuna,
  drained
3 cups of cooked and
  drained noodles
1 cup celery, chopped
  fine
½ cup Hellmann's
  mayonnaise
½ cup onion, chopped

⅓ cup green pepper,
  chopped
⅓ cup canned pimiento
  Salt and black pepper
1 can cream of celery
  soup
½ cup evaporated milk
  Some kind of good
  crunchy crumbs

Mix tuna fish, noodles, celery, mayonnaise, onion, green pepper, pimiento, and salt and pepper. Stir soup and milk until heated. Pour over tuna and put in a baking dish. Bake at 400 degrees for 25 minutes, uncovered. Then add crumbs and bake till brown (5 minutes).

WAY OUT THERE GRITS

2 cups cooked grits (off
  the stove)
2½ cups sharp yellow
  cheese
1 stick margarine

2 toes garlic, chopped
  fine
2 eggs
1 little hot green chili of
  some kind (chopped
  real fine)

Beat eggs and mix everything with the grits until the cheese has melted. Bake for 50 minutes at 350 degrees.
  Serves a plenty.

GERTRUDE SNIPE'S SNIPPY GRITS

1 cup grits, uncooked
1 log of garlic cheese,
   any kind
2 eggs
½ cup evaporated milk

1 stick margarine
Salt
1 cup crushed cereal,
   anything you got

Prepare grits according to box or bag. Melt the cheese (save a hunk) and the butter together then add to the grits. Beat milk with eggs and slowly stir into the grits. Salt to taste. Turn into a buttered baking dish, cover with crushed cereal. Grate the rest of the cheese on top of this and dot with lots of oleo. Bake at 350 degrees for 45–50 minutes.

    Serves six snippy ones.

AUNT JEANETTE BELLE PINK'S HOT & SASSY GRITS

2 cups cooking grits
1 cup of Jalapeno cheese,
   cubed
1½ cups Velveeta cheese,
   cut up

1 little onion, minced
1 stick of margarine
3 eggs

Cook grits according to directions. Stir in the cheeses, margarine and onion until melted. Beat the eggs and fold it into the mixture also. Pour in a greased baking dish. Bake at 325 degrees until the grits set up (about 50 minutes).

    Belle said, "You don't know whether you're havin a hot flash or not, when you eat this."

    Enough for about 6.

SUKI-WAWH-SUKI

4 cups already cooked
grits
½ lb loose sausage

2 cups cheese, melted
Buttered cracker
crumbs

Crumble the sausage and fry until brown. Pour off excess fat. Butter a baking dish and pour on half of the grits. Then add the sausage and half of the melted cheese. Cover with the rest of the grits and top with what's left of the cheese. Sprinkle cracker crumbs on the top. Bake for 20 minutes at 375 degrees.

"I don't know what this means but Jeanette Rose was justa screamin it one night while she was eatin this," Minna Dean swears.

BOILED PEANUTS

Wash your peanuts. (Hint for Yankees: don't shell.) Add one tablespoon salt to each quart of water and boil peanuts for 3 hours. They'll be soft and juicy on the inside and you won't be able to stop.

CAPTOLA'S RATTATOO-EE YOU ALL

2 large eggplants,
peeled, sliced in ¼
inch slices
Flour
Olive oil
8 medium zucchini
squash, cut into ½
inch pieces
5 large onions, thinly
sliced
6 garlic cloves, minced

6 large green bell
peppers, seeded,
diced
8 large tomatoes, peeled,
seeded, cut into strips
1 lb okra, washed and
sliced in ½ inch
slices
2 tsp thyme
2 tsp basil

Dredge eggplant slices lightly in flour and fry in olive oil over medium high heat for 5 minutes (don't crowd slices in the skillet). Drain on paper towels. Cook zucchini, onions, tomatoes, peppers, okra, garlic in the same oil until soft. Add more oil if you need it. Add the basil and thyme and blend. Layer eggplant slices and vegetables in a 6-quart baking dish. Bake, covered in a 350-degree oven for 45 minutes. Serve hot over soup bowls of crumbled corn bread.

If they ain't had a fit, they'll get one.

Serves 12.

AUNT AUDIE'S FISHY CHOWDER

1 lb frozen white fish fillets (cod, sole, haddock), thawed
1 small celery stick, sliced
2 onions, chopped
1 green pepper, chopped
2 cups potatoes, cut in chunks
5 cups Campbell's Chicken Broth
3 Tbs butter
3½ Tbs flour

Melt the butter in a pan. Add the onions and cook until soft, but not browned. Add flour and blend thoroughly. Add the chicken broth. Mix in the celery, potatoes, and peppers and season with salt and pepper to taste. Cook slowly for one hour. Add the thawed fish and cook another half hour.

"It's hard to kill a cravin, but this and biscuits'll sometimes do it," Aunt Audie said.

COOLIN OFF ICE TEA

Fill a small saucepan half full of water. Bring to boil and add a fistful of loose tea (if you can find it). Take off the fire and let sit a minute. In a tea pitcher strain the tea and squeeze all the juice out of it. Add water to the top and sweeten immediately. Serve on ice.

RACK OF SPAM

2 cans of Spam
10–12 cheese wedges

Cut the Spam in slices but don't go all the way through. You want it to open like a fan. Insert the cheese and bake at 400 till cheese is melted and the Spam is brown. Garnish with something.

WEENIES AND TORTELLINIS

½ pack wieners,
1 box tortellinis
1 cup coffee cream
2 Tbs flour

1 stick butter
Salt and pepper to taste
1 small bunch of broccoli

Chop weenies. Fix tortellinis. Cut broccoli into buds. Melt butter in a skillet. Add flour until smooth. Slowly pour in the cream. Add wennies, tortellinis, and broccoli and cook till sauce is thick and the broccoli is still bright green but tender.

TOMMIE KAY'S PEANUT BUTTER AND JELLY SOUP

½ cup chopped celery
½ cup green onions,
  finely chopped
  (including green tops)
4 Tbs margarine
2 Tbs flour
3 cups chicken broth,
  hot

¾ cup regular peanut
  butter
1 can evaporated milk
1 cup Jalapeno jelly
  (hottest you can find)
Salt and pepper

Fry onions and celery till limp but not brown in margarine. Sprinkle flour over them and stir to blend smoothly. Add chicken broth, stirring constantly. Beat in peanut butter, making sure the soup is very smooth. Season with salt and pepper. When you're going to serve the soup heat it up and quickly stir in the evaporated milk. You may not want to use it all. Make sure it doesn't boil though. Put a glob of jelly into the middle of each bowl and ladle on the soup.

BOILED COOKIES

2 cups sugar
½ cup milk
¼ lb butter or margarine
4 Tbs cocoa
2½ cups quick oatmeal
½ cup finely chopped nuts
2 tsp vanilla
½ cup crunchy peanut butter

Combine sugar, milk, butter, cocoa. Bring to rolling boil. Boil exactly one and a half minutes. Add remaining ingredients. Blend well. Press into a well greased square pan. Cool and cut into squares. Doesn't turn out too good on rainy days.

MINNA DEAN'S MOCK OYSTER DIP

1 Tbs onion, minced
1 stick butter
½ cup yellow cheese, grated
1 can cream of mushroom soup
1 small can mushroom pieces
1 package frozen chopped broccoli

Melt butter, add onion, fry until tender. Add cheese stirring until melted. Add soup and mushroom pieces. Cook 6 or 7 minutes. Cook broccoli first, drain and cool 10 minutes. Add to cheese mixture. Cook 10 minutes stirring occasionally. Serve with lots of saltines.

PAULETTE HUFF'S EASY GRASSHOPPER PIE

Crust:
6 oz chocolate wafer cookies
6 Tbs butter

Crush cookies and combine with melted butter. Press into a 9-inch pie pan.

Filling:
1½ cups whipping cream
1½ cups marshmallow
    creme
1½ oz green creme de
    menthe
½ oz creme de cacao

Combine whipped cream and softened marshmallow creme. Blend in liqueurs. Pour into pie shell and freeze at least 6 hours before serving.

LATE NIGHT DUMP CAKE

1 package yellow cake
    mix, any brand will
    do
1 1-lb can cherry pie
    filling
1 cup chopped pecans
1 1-lb can crushed
    pineapple in heavy
    syrup, undrained
1 stick of butter or
    margarine, sliced into
    thin pieces

Grease up a 9 x 13-inch pan. Spread pineapple in pan evenly. Spread cherry filling on top of pineapple evenly. Spread cake mix on top of cherry filling evenly. Put butter or margarine chips onto cake. Mix in some and sprinkle some with chopped nuts.

Bake at 350 degrees 40 to 50 minutes.

SUEULLA'S GOOFY BALLS

2 cups light brown sugar
1 cup plain flour
1 cup nuts
2 well beaten eggs

1 stick margarine
1 Tbs vanilla
confectioners sugar

Melt margarine, add other ingredients. Bake 20 minutes at 350 degrees in greased small brownie pan. Remove from oven, stir with spoon maybe twice. Do this in the next 5 or 10 minutes, or as the crust forms on top. Remove from oven while warm. Roll into small balls. Roll in confectioners sugar.

It makes you feel better just to make 'em.

DRY BEEF GRAVY

2½ oz dried beef
2 oz melted shortening

½ cup flour
1 quart sweet milk

Chop beef into fine pieces. Fry in shortening until slightly brown. Sift flour over beef and mix thoroughly. Add milk and stir constantly until thick. Serve over grits with toast or biscuits. Good for breakfast if you've got a crowd to feed.

SIMPLE SYRUP CANDY

1 large jar Alaga syrup (cane)
1 lb peanuts
3 Tbs oleo

Cook syrup and oleo over low to medium heat while peanuts are roasting in oven. Shell and skin peanuts and add to syrup. Cook over medium high heat until mixture forms a soft ball when dropped in cold water. Remove from stove and stir till you just can't wait any longer, then eat!

POTATO FIT CANDY

1 large potato   Powdered sugar
1 tsp vanilla   Peanut butter

Boil potato with jacket on, peel and mash. Add 1 teaspoon vanilla and powdered sugar until stiff like pie dough. Flour wax paper with powdered sugar. Turn candy onto paper and pat out. Spread with peanut butter, sprinkle with sugar. Roll up like a jelly roll and cut into slices.

ROSE PINK'S BALONEY ROLL-UPS

1 package baloney
1 carton orange juice
Plain yellow mustard

While standing in front of the refrigerator take one slice of baloney out of the package. Using the back of the package as your work area, tightly roll the baloney slice. Eat it and relish the salty taste or dip into the mustard and relish the salty taste! Now grab the orange juice carton and take a big swig . . . yes, straight from the carton. It's better that way. Repeat procedure until you can wait until lunch but you haven't lost your appetite. This snack is more enjoyable if, when eating, the refrigerator door is left open and you lean against the counter.

Minna Dean said, "When I found her propped-up in front of the icebox that night she still had mustard on her lips."

MAUD BOATRIGHT'S GARLICKY GRITS

4 cups milk
1 cup grits
½ cup oleo

1 6-oz roll garlic cheese
2 eggs
½ cup grated Cheddar cheese

Bring three and a half cups of the milk to boil. Gradually stir in grits. Cook until thick stirring for 10 minutes. Remove from heat. Add oleo and garlic cheese. Stir until melted. Stir in beaten eggs and remaining milk. Pour into 2-quart casserole. Bake at 325 degrees uncovered 30 minutes or until browned. Sprinkle Cheddar cheese over top and bake about 10 minutes longer.

EATIN ON
THE GROUND

AUNT DOE RAE'S PACKAGED-UP WORLD

Aunt Doe Rae was working her mind awful hard, trying to write up an announcement of this year's homecoming-and-dinner-on-the-ground for the New Mt. Nebo Creek Baptist Church. She, especially, was trying to find the language strong enough to put a stop to the onslaught of all the cardboard cartons and Styrofoam platters of food that could be bought at any corner convenient store. She was in tears thinking about last year's dinner and how it seems that almost everyone lost the feeling and the spirit of the dinner on the ground. She knew it would take some powerful words, but at this point she was willing to say anything she could to get this occasion back on the ground. She wrote and scratched for days until she had come up with what she considered some of the dos and don'ts for a homecoming dinner. It was mostly don'ts. When she had finished, she stood up at her kitchen table and began to read it out loud, as if the entire Mt. Nebo congregation was listening.

"Do any of you, or can any of you, remember when Nuvell was just Raenelle's twin-sister, plain ol, and not some skimpy kinda French cookin. I mean, last year at our dinner, I saw a three bean salad that consisted of egxactly that! Three beans, and a sprig of somethin that looked everbit like dogfennel to me. They a-fiddlin with our fat. That's what they doin. Now, I ain't advocatin unhealthy food but what can you say against Miss Lyddie's fried pork chops, she et 'em for 96 years. And she ain't never robbed, raped er murdered nobody. She did die, but it weren't her pork chops. She simply wore out. However, take the other fence, these young folks that's been a eatin all this messa enbombed cardboard since they was knee high, they are up to their eye-teeth in dope, akahal, an devilmint. I'll tell ya, it's got to be this fast, superized eatin, cause it ain't, no matter what they say, the coloreds, the communists, nor the poor ol kudzu vine. And cholesterol was nothin compared to the the repercussion of this soulless eatin.

"Anyways, it was a shameful sight last year, at our homecomin dinner. They was cartons and boxes on every tablecloth from all the fast food stores in the county. An not a one, an I mean, not a one had the decency to even cover 'em up with a nice piece of tinfoil er something. But ebem that wouldn'ta helped the taste none. Just, for instance, you take Viney's ol Chocolate Sheath Cake, she bakes it year after year after year, and then slips it down in a nest of foil on the bottom of any cutoff box. It ain't much. But, looks to high heaven. An'll melt in yo mouth, too. So you see, it... don't... TAKE ...much. I ain't askin for the sky. I'm just layin out the law this year. Not a one can bring a thing that they ain't cooked er made with their own two hands. Except for Miss Lucy, of course, she ain't got but one hand. It's got to come from your kitchen or you cain't bring it to the dinner. I don't care how many boxes and cans you use to make it, just so it come off your stove.

"Now, I'm aware that the Devil'll be workin overtime tryin to fool me, but I'll catch you, cause the Man Upstairs is gone be workin on my side. An you ladies out there, that works hard in your kitchens, I know I can depend on you to help me spot all that store-bought stuff and we'll throw it straight to the dawgs, where it belongs. Can you imagine seein Mrs. Bridie duMac's delicious Shoesoles and Grits sittin right nex ta a slice of some nasty frozen Pizza. Is that what we want our dinner affair to turn out to. No, it ain't!! An I'm puttin my foot right here to stop it. Now!! (She puts her foot out as if to trip somebody.) I know we ain't got no reason to go and get uppity about our food, cause we eat some pretty low...down...stuff ourselves. We not only eat the egg but there is them that eats "the where it come from". So, I know, we ain't fancy and we don't have all kinds a stuff that others has, but we'll take anything, and I do mean anything, an turn it till it hollers. An there is one thing you can always, just about, count on. FRESH. . . . . right off the stove, fresh. Everything from scratch, well, at least as much as you can get by with in this packaged-up world. You ain't got to mummafy food, if it's fresh made. Maybe, one warm-up, and then out it goes to the hawgs. So y'all, hear... me... good. It's them poisons in all the fast eatin that's caused this lack of pride, idle-handedness, and general no-count. It ain't the Fat. An, if I'm standin here as Aunt Doe Rae Dollar, I betcha ninety percent of them rapers, robbers and killers is skinny, skinny. An it ain't two of 'em that has ever said the blessin an eat on the ground."

AUNT DOE RAE'S RICE PUDDIN

1 cup uncooked rice
4 eggs
2 cans sweetened
    condensed milk

1 cup raisins
½ tsp ground nutmeg
2 Tbs vanilla

Make rice by package, fluffy and dry. Then mix it with the raisins and the milk in a pot sitting in hot water, kind of like a double boiler. Beat up the eggs (not too much) and slowly pour into the rice mixture, don't stop stirring whatever you do. Cook 6–8 minutes until it coats your spoon. Take off the fire and mix in vanilla and nutmeg. Now pour it into a dish you can take with you and shower it lightly with some more nutmeg.
    Serves 12.

CALLEEN'S CHICKEN FRIED RABBIT AND GRAVY

1 frying rabbit, cut into
    pieces
1 cup flour

1 tsp salt
½ tsp pepper
1 cup Crisco

Mix together the flour, salt, and pepper in a brown paper bag. Put rabbit pieces into the flour bag, a few at a time and shake, coating them completely before frying. Heat Crisco in an iron skillet and add the rabbit pieces (do not overcrowd the skillet) and brown well on both sides. Reduce heat and cook, turning once more. Drain all but 3 tablespoons of the grease from the skillet. Add about a half cup flour and brown it, stirring and scraping up the brown bits from the bottom of the skillet. When the mixture is browned, add one and a half cups water slowly, stirring. Cook over low heat until gravy is thick.

FRIED MEAT, SAWMILL GRAVY, AND CATHEAD BISCUITS

Wash a pound or so of salt pork and slice to a quarter inch. Put in a black iron skillet and cover with water and bring to a boil. Drain the meat and rinse again to get rid of what's left of the salt. Then cook the salt pork in the skillet, slowly, until golden brown. Drain on paper. Pour off all but two or three tablespoons of the grease from the skillet and turn the heat up to medium. Add about three tablespoons of flour and brown. Mix a quarter cup of water and three fourths cup of milk. Add slowly to the skillet, stirring constantly. Salt and pepper it to taste and bring to a boil at medium heat. Good served over hot Cathead Biscuits.

CATHEAD BISCUITS

2 cups White Lily self-rising flour
½ cup lard
¾ cup buttermilk

Cut in shortening till it looks like meal. Add enough milk to make the dough come away from the sides of the bowl. Knead on a floured surface 10 or more times. Pinch off 6 to 8 good-size pieces and roll into biscuits no more that three quarters inch thick. Place on an ungreased baking tin and put in a preheated 450-degree oven for 15 minutes or until golden brown and big as cat heads.

Make your biscuit, meat and gravy sandwiches before you leave home. They'll be good and juicy by the time they're served.

Will serve four or more, depending on their appetites.

FRIED CORN

9 fresh corn ears
½ cup bacon drippings
1 cup half and half cream
(sweet milk will do)

Salt and pepper to your
taste

With a sharp knife run down the cob and slice off all the corn.
Then scrape the cob until all the corn juice is removed. Into a hot
black iron skillet add the drippings. When it sizzles add the corn
stirring a lot so it doesn't stick or burn, but it should get a little
crispy. Cook till thick (6 or 7 minutes), don't stop stirring. Pour in
the cream, salt, pepper. Put a lid on it and cook slow for 10 to 15
minutes more. Cool it and take it right on to the dinner.
    Serves 4.

MISS QUEEN'S CRACKLIN CORN BREAD

2 cups self-rising
    cornmeal
1½ cups buttermilk
1 egg

1 Tbs melted Crisco
1 cup cracklins or crispy
    fried bacon crumbs

Add the buttermilk and egg to the cornmeal, stirring until
blended. Fold in cracklins and half of the Crisco. Pour batter into
a sizzling hot, well greased skillet (the one with the rest of the
melted Crisco). Bake at 450 degrees for 25 minutes. Wrap it up
good to keep it hot!
    Will serve 6.

RACHEL MOODY'S FRIED CHICKEN WITH MILK CREAM GRAVY

1 2½-lb fryer, cut up
1 cup flour
1 tsp salt

¼ tsp pepper
1½ cups butter-flavored
    shortening

Put flour, salt, and pepper in a grocery bag. Drop in the chicken, roll up the bag and shake until all pieces are coated. Make sure to hold a hand on the bottom of the bag. Heat shortening in an iron skillet and place the pieces of chicken into the hot fat (careful not to splash the grease), turning often to brown. After browning the chicken, cover skillet and cook about 20 minutes. Remove the lid and cook another 10 minutes. Drain on paper towels. Serve with Milk Cream Gravy.

To make milk cream gravy: drain off the fat from the skillet, except for five tablespoons, saving all the crispies. Stir in two or three tablespoons of flour till smooth. Slowly add two cups of milk. Stir and thicken. Salt and pepper to taste.

Sometimes I pour my gravy right over the chicken in the skillet. There's always a batch of biscuits or cake of corn bread to sop it up.

MARTHIE'S MT. NEBO DRESSED CHICKEN

2 lbs cooked and boned
    chicken meat
½ stick oleo
1 box corn bread stuffing
    mix
½ cup evaporated milk

1 can cream of celery
    soup
1½ cups chicken broth
    (saved from the boiled
    chicken)

Put chicken meat in a deep cast iron Dutch oven or other pot. In a saucepan melt oleo and combine with soup and milk till hot. Pour over the chicken. Mix the corn bread stuffing with the chicken broth and spoon over the chicken mixture in the Dutch oven while it is on the fire. Don't stir it up. Bake for 25 minutes in 425-degree oven or until the dressing is brown.

Make certain you take a big spoon to dish it out.

TURNIP GREENS, POT LIKKER, AND CORNMEAL DODGERS

2 bunches turnip greens
2 quarts cold water

½ lb chopped country
 ham
1 Tbs oil

Fry ham in a pot large enough to hold all the greens. Wash turnip greens in two or three waters (to git rid of the grit). Cut off tough stems, bruised and wilted leaves. Add the greens to the frying ham and cook covered until completely wilted and seared on the bottom. Add 2 quarts of water and slow boil till greens are tender (30 or 40 minutes). Season the greens with salt and pepper to taste and keep hot on stove until dodgers are ready to cook.

Cornmeal dodgers: mix 1 cup white self-rising cornmeal and a half teaspoon salt. Cut in two tablespoons melted shortening. Slowly mix four or five tablespoons cold water until it makes a dough that can hold its own shape. Make biscuit size dodgers and gently lay on top of the boiling pot likker and greens. Bring up to a boil, turn down the heat, put a lid on and simmer about 20 minutes.

Makes 6 dodgers.

FRANCEEN'S GOOD OL MEAT

1 can Spam Cracker crumbs (saltines, of course)	2 beaten eggs Crisco and butter (or just either one)

Slice Spam into 6 or 8 pieces. Roll in finely crushed crumbs and then into egg and back in crumbs again, pressing firmly. Let sit awhile. Melt shortening and/or butter in skillet and fry Spam slices until golden, turning once or twice. Good with ketchup or chili sauce. Serve hot. Cold leftovers make good sandwiches with white bread and Miracle Whip.

Franceen Jance said she's seen 'em sneak these into the Kentucky Derby when she lived there.

MISS FAITH RIVER'S PLEASIN PAPPY CAKE

The reason this is called a 'Pleasin Pappy Cake' is because it makes such a good, sturdy batter. So, whatever cake pleases Pappy you can bake him in a jiffy, by just shifting around the ingredients. Strawberries, chocolate, apples. You name it!

Basic Cake:

2 eggs 10 Tbs butter 1⅔ cups sugar 2¾ cups plain flour	1½ tsp baking powder 1 tsp vanilla 1¼ cups milk

Soften the butter, then cream with sugar. Add eggs. Add baking powder, vanilla, and then mix in the flour and the milk, a little of each at a time till all used up. Beat till it looks smooth. Pour into two layer pans, or tube pan, or one 9 x 12-inch pan, that has been greased and floured. Bake at 350 degrees till lightly browned and knife comes out clean when stuck in middle of cake.

Icing:

1 box 10X powdered
  sugar
1 stick butter

1 tsp vanilla or almond
  flavoring
A little bit of milk

Mix first three ingredients and enough milk to make it look like icing. Spread on cooled cake.

For strawberry cake, add half or a third a carton frozen strawberries. Put the rest of them in the icing, but leave off the milk, use some of the juice for liquid. Add some extra sugar if you think it needs it. For chocolate cake, mix in 3 or 4 melted squares of semi-sweet chocolate or 3 to 4 tablespoons of cocoa. Same amount of melted squares or cocoa for the icing. Pappy wants an apple cake? Then stir two cups thinly sliced apples and one cup finely chopped walnuts into the batter. Makes a delicious moist cake. Ice it with half cup butter and a package of cream cheese, an eight ounce one, all whomped up with some chopped walnuts too.

BEE BEE FLICK'S COVERED DISH CHICKEN

Meat from 1 cooked
  and boned chicken,
  chopped
2 cups cooked rice
4 celery stalks, chopped
1 small yellow onion,
  chopped
1 cup mayonnaise
3 hard-boiled eggs,
  chopped

2 cans Campbell's
  Golden Mushroom
  Soup
½ cup pecans, chopped
1 Tbs French's mustard
1 cup cracker crumbs
1 tsp salt
2 Tbs melted margarine

In a casserole dish mix everything except bread crumbs and melted margarine. Stir together the bread crumbs and the melted butter and sprinkle over the top of the casserole and bake at 350 degrees for 40 minutes or until it bubbles.

HILLIE'S LEMON CHESS PIE

3 eggs, well beaten
1 stick of butter
1½ cups of sugar
1 Tbs cornmeal

1 Tbs white vinegar
1 tsp lemon extract
Pie crust, uncooked

Cream butter and sugar. Then stir in cornmeal and eggs. Add flavoring and vinegar. Pour into pie crust and bake at 350 degrees until firm.

Hillie Manes says this is so good it'll make you drop yo drawers.

JW'S DOUBLE CHEESE CASSEROLE

1 lb sharp grated
   Cheddar cheese
1 lb cottage cheese
6 eggs, beaten
¼ tsp nutmeg
¼ tsp cayenne pepper
1 cup Bisquick

1 garlic clove, pressed
1 cube chicken bouillon
½ cup dry, not sweet,
   sherry wine
½ cup milk
½ cup melted butter

Mix together the cheeses and eggs. Add the cayenne, nutmeg, garlic, and Bisquick to the cheese mixture and blend thoroughly. Heat, but don't boil the sherry wine and dissolve the chicken bouillon cube. Mix the sherry mixture with the milk and add to the cheese mixture. Pour half the melted butter into a casserole and add the other half to the cheese mixture and blend thoroughly. Pour into the casserole and bake for 40 minutes in a 350-degree oven.

Serves 6.

VADA MILDRED'S PAN FRIED MULLET

Clean and scale the mullet but leave him whole. Any pan-size fish will do. Salt, pepper and a little bit of cornmeal on each side.

On an open fire heat up the black iron skillet with a good amount of grease in it. When it's hot drop in the mullet and fry until crispy and brown. Drown him in lemon juice and serve.

Aunt Doe Rae said, "Vada did this right at the dinner and they come all the way from Jawga for 'em."

MISS LYDDIE'S FRIED PORK CHOPS

12 pork chops, rubbed with a small amount of brown sugar
Salt and pepper to taste
Flour (enough to cover them good)

Heat Crisco shortening in a cast iron skillet and fry the chops to a golden brown. Pile up on a platter, cover and they are ready to go to the dinner.

MARY LOU GURR'S THUMP SALAD

4 cups mashed potatoes, leftover, seasoned and a little dry
¼ cup diced celery
¼ cup diced green pepper
¼ cup diced onion or scallions

2 hard-boiled yard eggs, chopped
5 or 6 Tbs of mayonnaise
3 tsp mustard

Mix potatoes, mayonnaise and mustard thoroughly. Fold in the celery, peppers, and onions. Then the eggs (eggs last so as not to mash the yolks). Taste for seasoning. Add more mayonnaise if it's too dry. Best served at room temperature or you can chill it.

TWO DINNER BEEF STEW POT PIE

2 lbs of stew beef	3 medium potatoes
2 Tbs shortening	Flour
1 large onion	Salt and pepper
3 carrots	

Dredge salted and peppered beef in flour. Fry in shortening until brown. Add enough water to cover. Turn down heat, put a lid on and cook meat until tender. Add onions, carrots, and potatoes and again cover with water. Cook until vegetables are like you like them. Salt and pepper to taste. Serve.

POT PIE

Take what's left of the beef stew and add a package of frozen peas to it. Sometimes you need a little more juice too. Heat it up on the stove to a bubble. Cover with homemade biscuits and put in hot oven for 10 or 20 minutes (when the biscuits are brown).

Biscuit Dough:
2 cups self-rising flour
¼ cup lard
Sweet milk

Cut lard into the flour until it looks like a coarse meal. Add a little milk at the time, enough to make a thick dough. Roll out on a floured surface and cut biscuits with the end of a Calumet can.

ROOSTER AND DUMPLINS

Kill and dress the rooster. Cut in pieces and put in a pot that has a cover. Cover with water. Add one teaspoon salt and a half teaspoon of black pepper, more if you like it. Cover and stew slowly until the meat begins to fall off the bone. Take out the meat and remove the bones. Add enough flour dissolved in water to thicken the broth. Then return the meat to the pot.

Dumplins:

2 cups flour
4 tsp baking powder
   Milk

2 Tbs rooster fat
   (skimmed from the
   pot)
½ tsp salt

Mix flour, salt and baking powder. Cut in the fat with a fork or something. Add milk a little at the time until a thick drop batter is formed. Spoon onto the boiling chicken until dough is all gone. Cover and boil for 12 minutes. It takes that steam to cook little fluffy dumplins. Drop by tablespoon if you like big ones and a teaspoon if you like little ones. Take it right off the stove and put it on the back seat and head for the dinner. It's also good for company comin.

AUNT MILDRED'S MUSTARDS

2 bunches of mustard
   greens
   Lean ham hunks

3 chicken bouillon cubes
   Salt and pepper to taste

Rip all the leaves from the stems and wash at least 3 times maybe more. If you miss a stem here and there, don't worry, some people like a little stem. Fry the ham hunks in a big pot and put in the mustards. When they are all wilted, add water to cover, bouillon and cook till tender.

"They not so fatty," Aunt Mildred said.

AUNT DOE RAE'S BUTTERMILK POUND CAKE

1 cup shortening
2 cups sugar
4 eggs
2½ cups plain flour

½ cup self-rising flour
1 cup milk
1 Tbs butternut flavoring

Cream shortening, sugar and eggs for one minute. Blend flours. Add half of flour to creamed mixture. Beat one minute. Add milk and remaining flour. Add flavoring and beat well. Bake at 325 degrees for one hour. Increase heat to 350 degrees and bake 10 minutes more.

Icing:
1 box powdered sugar
½ cup shortening
1 Tbs butternut flavoring

Blend sugar and shortening. Add flavoring. Add enough milk to make it easy to spread out icing on cooled cake.

BRIDIE DUMAC'S SHOESOLES AND GRITS

3 or 4 thin cubed steaks the
size of a shoesole
1 small onion, chopped

1 can stewed tomatoes
4 cups cooked grits

Flour and fry steaks. Cook down onions and tomato. Make grits by directions on bag. Grease a glass loaf dish and put a layer of grits and a steak and a layer of tomatoes. Repeat till gone. Top with grits. Let sit till firm and slice like meat loaf.

PREACHER'S WIFE'S BUTTERSCOTCH DESSERT

First layer:
1 cup flour
1 stick butter
½ cup chopped pecans

Mix together and press into 9 x 13-inch pan or two pie shells. Bake at 325 degrees for 15 minutes. Then cool.

Second layer:
1 8-oz package cream cheese
1 cup powdered sugar
1 cup Cool Whip

Beat well the cream cheese and sugar, then add Cool Whip and spread onto first layer.

Third layer:
1 package instant vanilla pudding
1 package instant butterscotch pudding
3 cups milk
1 Tbs vanilla

Mix well and let stand until thick and spread over second layer. Top with more Cool Whip and refrigerate.

This was not accepted at Mt. Nebo when she first come here.

VINEY'S CHOCOLATE SHEATH CAKE

2 cups sugar
2 cups self-rising flour
1 stick oleo
½ cup oil
4 Tbs cocoa
1 cup milk

½ cup buttermilk
2 eggs
½ tsp cinnamon
2 pinches salt
1 Tbs vanilla

Sift together sugar and flour into large bowl. Place oleo, oil, and cocoa, milk into saucepan. Bring to rapid boil. Pour over flour and sugar, beating well. Mix together buttermilk, eggs, cinnamon, salt, and vanilla and pour into other mixture. Mix well and put into greased pan. Bake at 400 degrees for 20 minutes.

Icing:

½ cup nuts
1 tsp vanilla
1 stick oleo

6 Tbs milk
4 Tbs cocoa
1 box powdered sugar

Put all ingredients except sugar in saucepan and bring to slow boil. Add sugar and spread on cake while it is still warm.

WORKING GIRL'S CASSEROLE

6 medium potatoes
1 cup grated cheese

1 lb hamburger
½ cup chopped onion

Cook and mash potatoes till creamy. Put in a casserole and using spoon hollow out hole in center about the size of a saucer. Brown loose hamburger and onions. Fill hole in potatoes with hamburger and onions. Cover with grated cheese. Place in oven at 450 degrees until cheese melts and is bubbly and you're ready to eat. It travels good too.

GRAMMA WHITT'S FAMOUS FLAP JACK

2 cups self-rising flour
½ tsp soda
¼ tsp sugar

2 Tbs Crisco shortening
1½ cups buttermilk

Sift dry ingredients into a mixing bowl. Mix well. Add buttermilk and shortening. Stir until the liquid is mixed enough to pour the batter into a greased pan. Bake at 400 degrees until brown.

She just takes a big platter of them to the dinner and serves 'em with milk gravy.

LYNN WOOD'S COMPANY CHICKEN

A cut-up chicken
Flour
Salt and pepper
Apple, sliced
Green peppers, sliced

Onion, chopped
White raisins
Butter
White wine
Slivered almonds

Dredge chicken in flour, season with salt and pepper, and fry until nice and brown. Put in a casserole in layers with the apples, onions, and green peppers. Pour over all this some white wine, enough that you can just see it below the top layer. Dot with hunks of butter. Top with almonds. Cook covered in oven at 375 degrees for an hour. Uncover and cook another 15 minutes to brown almonds.

Lynn said, "It's better if you fix it the day before and let it sit in the icebox overnight then heat it up for your company."

VINEY'S VINEGAR PIE

1 stick margarine,
   melted and cooled
2 Tbs flour
1½ cups sugar

1 Tbs vanilla
2 Tbs vinegar
3 whole eggs
1 9-inch baked pie shell

Combine margarine, vanilla, sugar, flour, vinegar, and eggs. Pour into pie shell. Bake at 300 degrees for 45 minutes.

INDEX

LITTLE EXTRAS